# MEDIUMSHIP

*Sacred Communications with
Loved Ones from Across the Veil*

Enjoy these other books in the Common Sentience series:

**AKASHA:** *Spiritual Experiences of Accessing the Infinite Intelligence of Our Souls*

**ANCESTORS:** *Divine Remembrances of Lineage, Relations and Sacred Sites*

**ANGELS:** *Personal Encounters with Divine Beings of Light*

**ANIMALS:** *Personal Tales of Encounters with Spirit Animals*

**ASCENSION:** *Divine Stories of Awakening the Whole and Holy Being Within*

**GODDESS:** *Blessed Reunions with the Feminine Face of the Divine*

**GODTALK:** *Experiences of Humanity's Connections with a Higher Power*

**GUIDES:** *Mystical Connections to Soul Guides and Divine Teachers*

**MEDITATION:** *Intimate Experiences with the Divine through Contemplative Practices*

**NATURE:** *Divine Experiences with Trees, Plants, Stones and Landscapes*

**PORTALS:** *Energetic Doorways to Mystical Experiences Between Worlds*

**SHAMANISM:** *Personal Quests of Communion with Nature and Creation*

**SIGNS:** *Sacred Encounters with Pathways, Turning Points, and Divine Guideposts*

**SOUND:** *Profound Experiences with Chanting, Toning, Music and Healing Frequencies*

**WITCH:** *Divine Alignments with the Primordial Energies of Magick and Cycles of Nature*

Learn more at sacredstories.com

# MEDIUMSHIP

*Sacred Communications with*
*Loved Ones from Across the Veil*

## SUZANNE GIESEMANN

Books may be purchased through booksellers or by contacting Sacred Stories Publishing.

Mediumship
Sacred Communications with Loved Ones from Across the Veil

Suzanne Giesemann

Print ISBN: 978-1-958921-60-9
EBook ISBN: 978-1-958921-61-6

Library of Congress Control Number: 2024932669

Published by Sacred Stories Publishing, Fort Lauderdale, FL USA

# CONTENTS

## PART THREE: DEEPENING YOUR CONNECTION WITH THE DIVINE

## MEET THE SACRED STORYTELLERS
## MEET THE AUTHOR

# PART ONE

*Understanding Mediumship*

*The connection with your loved ones who have passed is far more than a memory. It is ongoing.*

— SANAYA, SUZANNE'S GUIDES

# SERVING THE TWO WORLDS

t's not easy being human. Life is filled with ups and downs. One of the greatest challenges in any lifetime is dealing with the death of someone close. The thought of never again seeing someone you love can be unbearable.

But what if death is not the end? What if those who have passed still exist, albeit in a different form? What if they are as close as your breath, free of pain and suffering, aware of your thoughts and actions? What if you could establish an ongoing relationship with loved ones across the veil, consciously aware of their presence, and move forward knowing they move forward with you?

This may sound like wishful thinking or a fairy tale, but I can assure you that all of these scenarios describe reality that is revealed through mediumship. Communications with those who have passed show that death is not the end, but the turning of a page to another chapter in the eternal life of the soul.

Mediumistic encounters reveal the presence of sentient, clever, and creative beings. They show that those in spirit are still very much people, even though they are no longer experiencing life with a physical body.

It can be immensely healing to hear from those you thought were dead and forever gone from your life. One brief but meaningful encounter with someone across the veil can change your worldview in an instant and greatly relieve the pain and sadness of grief.

An equally important and life-changing lesson learned from mediumship is that this earthly realm is not the only reality. Through transdimensional communication, you discover that you are part of one multidimensional web connecting all that is. Taken to the greatest realization of all, you realize that these non-physical interactions are possible because you are a direct expression of one omnipresent, omnipotent, omniscient, and all-loving Source.

The information, stories, and methods in this transformative book will redirect you to a greater understanding of your soul's journey of awakening and your role in a larger reality than we experience on Earth. As you educate yourself and engage higher consciousness for your unique purposes, you will realize that the more spacious aspect of your self—your soul—exists right here, right now, at a level beyond your human challenges. You may very well come to know, beyond any doubt, what you as a soul have never forgotten: That death is not something to be feared, but merely a transition to another state of consciousness.

This is all tremendously welcome news! And yet, despite the clear and convincing evidence from ethical mediums practicing for hundreds of years, mediumship is only now becoming accepted as a legitimate practice.

The benefits that embracing mediumship provides are profound. Its healing potential and the opportunities for spiritual growth can be seen by contrasting skeptics and those steeped in fear-based dogma with believers in an interactive afterlife.

A case in point is some bereavement support groups do not allow open discussions of the afterlife. Their members often find that, despite attending many meetings, they remain as stuck in their grief as when their loved one first passed. Meetings can be depressing events that only accentuate the pain from the false belief that they will never see their loved one again.

Contrast this with a different kind of bereavement group in which mediumship plays a key role. In these groups, as a result of communicating with their loved ones in spirit, individuals are aided in making the shift from a state of grief and emotional heaviness to one of hopefulness and peace of mind. Regardless of one's religious or non-religious background, all individuals are welcomed, and recovery is fueled by a non-dogmatic approach to spiritual experiences and evidence of an afterlife.

While it is wise to question claims of connecting with the deceased, there is a difference between close-minded and open-minded skepticism. Being close-minded leaves no room for discovery and growth. Those who are open to the possibility of spirit communication welcome new information and unique experiences that can result in an expanded world view and personal transformation.

I had heard about mediumship, but I never had any interest or reason to visit a medium until my stepdaughter, Susan—a sergeant in the U.S. Marines—was struck and killed by lightning while crossing the flight line at the air station where she was assigned. She was twenty-seven. Devastated by her passing, I was stunned when I saw her lifeless body in the coffin at the funeral home.

"That's not Susan. That is not Susan!" I repeated over and over, because it was inconceivable that the bright, lively young woman I loved could have simply disappeared. How could all that energy and love vanish?

I had been raised with no religion and had no belief in a heaven with angels cavorting in the clouds. But Susan had been so vibrant—so *alive.* In that gut-wrenching moment, I realized something important. I knew that what people called a spirit or a soul must be what enlivens the body, for this spark was so clearly missing from Susan now.

I vowed that if Susan still existed in some form, I would learn to connect with her myself.

I had heard about people who could naturally sense deceased loved ones, but I knew little about their work. I set the goal of learning more about the afterlife and finding a legitimate medium while doing whatever it took to establish personal contact.

Sensitive to the fact that anyone who Googled our last name would find the tribute to Susan that I had posted online, and aware of our vulnerable state, I did not want to risk being duped by a charlatan. When I found a medium who I felt was genuine and trustworthy, I deliberately withheld our identity. I regret now that I had such distrust, but I acknowledge the human tendency to question things we can't detect with our physical senses.

I needn't have doubted the wonderful medium who answered my prayers. During a life-changing session, Sophy showed my husband Ty and me that I had been correct in sensing that Susan's bright light could not possibly be extinguished.

Over the course of one hour, she left no doubt that Susan was in the room with us. She sensed a young woman in her twenties who passed suddenly, giving her a tingly, electrical feeling up and down her arms. Sophy had no idea that Susan had been killed by lightning.

She described this woman wearing a brown uniform, calling my husband Daddy, and sitting on his lap with her arms around his neck. Despite being a tough-as-nails military sergeant, Susan had always been a daddy's girl. She frequently plopped herself onto Ty's lap exactly as Sophy saw—and even more significantly, this was exactly the way she bid Ty goodbye the last time we saw her.

The clincher was when Sophy told us that the young woman had a baby boy with her who she wanted to introduce to us. At this point, both Ty and I were sobbing with a blend of disbelief and relief. The medium had no way of knowing that Susan had been six months pregnant with a boy when she was killed.

I sat there in shock, thinking, *You mean this is real? She really is here?*

There was no explanation for the things Sophy shared with us. Neither could we explain how a large, potted plant on the coffee table between us suddenly fell onto the floor by itself and shattered, mid-session, defying the laws of this physical universe.

In the seven months prior to this mediumship session, I had slogged through each day numbed by a foggy state of depression. Sessions with counselors who had no idea how it felt to deal with the death of a child had done nothing to ease my pain.

But now, thanks to that evidence-based session with a medium, we went from hoping that Susan still existed to *knowing* that the afterlife is real and that she is with us.

I had asked for evidence to prove Susan was there and we got it, in spades. To be sure, we still miss her, and we always will—but in that medium's office, the fog cleared, and our lives were forever changed.

This is the healing power of mediumship.

# A GREATER REALITY

ediumship is multi-faceted and involves real-time, planned and unplanned interactions with those in the spirit world. It also includes what are known as *after death communications* (ADCs) such as dream visits, signs, sensations, and even physical apparitions from those who have passed.

For centuries, ordinary people and well-known historical figures have been documented communicating with those in the spirit world. In the 1400s, Joan of Arc claimed that discarnate voices gave her the order to lead her fellow Frenchmen to victory against the British. In the 1700s, the theologian, scientist, and philosopher Emanual Swedenborg spoke openly about the spirit world as a separate realm.

In the mid-1800s, President Lincoln brought mediums into the White House to contact his deceased son. Around the same time, the Fox sisters in Hydesville, New York, established themselves as pioneers of the Modern Spiritualist movement by receiving mediumistic communication in the form of rapping from a man whose body was later discovered to have been buried in their house.

Well-educated scientists such as William James and J.B. Rhine formed psychical research organizations to investigate mediumship and other paranormal phenomena at the end of the nineteenth century in the United States and England. Similar groups, such as the Institute of Noetic Sciences and the Windbridge Research Center continue studies to this day, and a number of reputable university departments of consciousness studies still investigate "dying, death, and what comes next."

Such efforts bring scientific rigor to the study of experiences that cannot be explained solely through the physical senses. Thanks to these dedicated pioneers, the *paranormal* is now more frequently being accepted as perfectly normal. Thanks to what I call 21ˢᵗ Century Spirituality™, scientists are coming to understand what sages have known throughout the ages: What we call the objective, physical world is not the only reality.

Two of the most critical discoveries in quantum physics relate directly to mediumship. The first is that when we closely examine physical matter and attempt to research objects smaller than the tiniest bits, matter simply dissolves into waves of possibility. This shows us that there is a reality beyond space and time. Mediumship allows us to explore these alternate dimensions with the mind.

The second discovery is that entanglement is real. The Nobel prize in physics was awarded in 2022 for experiments that proved that once two particles have been connected, they react to each other not at the speed of light, but instantaneously. This discovery confirmed what mediumship also reveals: At the quantum level, everything is connected.

Materialists insist that the brain creates consciousness. Science has now shown what mediums experience firsthand each time they communicate with non-physical beings who have survived the death of the body: The brain does not create consciousness, and we do not cease to exist when the body dies.

There is a greater reality than this physical world. We are multidimensional beings existing in a limitless cosmos where consciousness is the fundamental reality.

## WHAT IS A MEDIUM?

Mediums serve as intermediaries between those in the physical and non-physical worlds. They provide a voice for those who no longer have vocal cords, lips, and a tongue to speak. To be sure, unethical people purporting to be mediums do exist. There are practitioners in every helping vocation who will take advantage of those who are hurting and vulnerable.

Legitimate evidence-based mediums, however, are far easier to find today than in the past. Thanks to the internet and organizations that train, test, and verify paranormal abilities, mediumship is becoming more mainstream and accepted as a trusted healing modality.

Contrary to what many believe, mediumship is not restricted to those who were born with this gift and have been seeing and communicating with spirits since childhood. I am a prime example of someone who did not know until I was in my mid-forties that the spirit world exists.

The stunning revelations from my first reading when Susan came through compelled me to learn as much as I could about mediumship and the afterlife. In the process of diving into the world of mediums, I discovered that I had the ability to connect with Susan and others' loved ones. Having enjoyed a full career as a naval officer and serving at the top level of the United States military, this was quite an unexpected development!

I immediately felt a calling to help others who were grieving to find hope, as our family had. I dedicated the following years to honing my skills to the best of my ability, and I continue to do so, for mediumship is an ongoing journey of discovery and improvement.

At my husband's urging, some years back, I began teaching the methods that work best. I have now trained thousands of people from diverse backgrounds to practice mediumship. Not everyone is called to do readings for others and engage in the kind of clear, two-way conversations with those in spirit as a professional medium. I know with deep certainty, however, that because we are souls in human form, we all have the latent ability to enjoy what I call personal mediumship.

By practicing the same methods as professionals, you can increase the possibility of connecting directly with your own loved ones during planned sessions when you sit with the intention of doing so.

You can also learn to recognize the after death communications (ADCs) our loved ones employ to let us know they are present. These are often spontaneous and unplanned. Part 2 of this book includes some powerful examples of irrefutable ADCs. Each story speaks to the universality of grief and love. Each also provides immense promise.

Whether an ADC or two-way communications, both styles fulfill the main goals of mediumship:

- To prove the continuity of consciousness beyond physical death
- To remind us who we are as souls temporarily in physical bodies
- To show us how interconnected the physical and non-physical worlds are

Part 3 introduces several practices that will increase the possibility of you having mediumistic experiences. The degree to which you develop this ability depends upon your commitment, perseverance, and whether you view mediumship as a curiosity or a calling.

Medium Anne Gehman once told me that practicing mediumship is like playing the piano. Everyone can learn to play a song or two, but not everyone is born to be a Mozart. Some are satisfied to leave mediumship to the professionals and may enjoy a brief personal connection with deceased loved ones by grace. Sometimes, that's all we need until we meet again, face to face.

At the other end of the spectrum are those who see spirits easily and need no specific practices to discern their presence. They are the "Mozarts." Those of us in the middle might need to practice our scales over and over, but the rewards far outweigh the effort.

No matter which way you enjoy mediumship, we are all part of one symphony and one greater reality. Your loved ones in the spirit world are eager to let you know they are here.

# SPIRIT WITH A CAPITAL S

One challenge in discussing mediumship is agreeing about the terms we use. Two often misunderstood terms are *soul* and *spirit*. The definitions which follow might differ from what you have learned. By explaining my perspective, I hope to remove any confusion and expand your understanding of these amorphous concepts.

Spirit—with a capital S—is the foundational core of all experience. Spirit is synonymous with Consciousness or Life Force and the many other words and phrases we use to describe the formless, fundamental essence of what I refer to as LIFE: Love in Full Expression.

We can speak of *spirit* without capitalizing it to refer to the life force that animates a certain person, animal, or other living thing, whether in a body or not. This spirit arises from the one true Spirit.

When we speak of "a spirit," we are referring to an individuated expression of Spirit that is not in a physical body. A spirit can be an angel, an archangel, or any of the limitless, non-physical forms that Spirit can take, including our loved ones who have passed. We call these *spirit beings*.

Consciousness, or Spirit, in its purest sense, is limitless—the All That Is. When it expresses anything other than its boundless nature, it limits itself for a particular experience. This is why I differentiate between *big-C* Consciousness and *little-c* consciousness. All that exists is big-C Consciousness expressing itself as and through an infinite variety of forms. You and I and those across the veil are all little-c consciousness. This interconnectedness is what makes connections in mediumship possible.

Consciousness expresses itself across a spectrum of self-awareness. This awareness can be restricted, such as in a plant or an insect, or it can be more self-aware, such as in a human being. Self-awareness becomes far less restricted as Consciousness expresses itself through what we call *higher beings*.

To understand the nature of Spirit expressing itself through various forms and dimensions, picture a set of Russian nested dolls. Spirit or Source would encompass all levels. The soul would be one of the dolls within the nest. Your higher self is yet another doll nested within the soul doll. It represents a particular lifetime or one role of many that the soul can project.

Your higher self encompasses the physical body and the layers of non-physical bodies associated with it. These include the mental, emotional, and spiritual bodies that make up what I call "The Story of You." The higher self does not die when the body no longer functions. It remains part of the soul for all eternity. The soul is spacious enough to contain the story of countless lifetimes or higher selves.

The axiom "As above, so below" is appropriate when trying to understand the relationship between Spirit and the spirit beings which arise from It. In addition to the nested doll analogy, you may picture Source like one flowing sea of consciousness. The soul is a whirlpool or eddy of energy-information within this limitless sea, and each soul—being a spin-off of this sentient, creative Source—whirls its own unique eddies of energy-information.

You are the spin-off of a soul. You are a sentient, creative being with a vast lineage of being the light of consciousness in expression. All LIFE is interconnected. You are playing a role that the soul chose to enact for the fullness of the human experience.

After you shed your human body at the transition we call death, you—the soul—choose to continue playing the role in the non-physical realm for as long as it serves the greater good. It is this field of energy-information that a medium attunes to when communicating soul-to-soul.

To call our loved ones who have died a "field of energy-information" may feel impersonal and non-loving. Don't worry, you are comprised of this same energy-information right now as you walk about in a body.

The personal part of you as a human and as a soul is inherent in your true nature as an expression of Source. The energy and information that forms your unique swirl of consciousness is intelligent, creative, clever, humorous, and all the other attributes that reflect your innate divinity. Humans who don't seem particularly Divine are simply blind to their deepest essence.

As we wrap up this discussion of terminology, please be clear about one critical point: You do not *have* a soul—you *are* a soul having a human experience. The person you call *me* is the limited aspect of a much less-constricted soul. Your human experiences may at times cause you to feel less than, but you as a soul are always and already whole and complete.

You did not incarnate to learn lessons because there is something wrong with your soul. You, a beautiful, shining light, took on the human experience to add to something that is already magnificent!

## PSYCHIC WORK VS. MEDIUMSHIP

Many students of mediumship have heard the phrase, "All mediums are psychic, but not all psychics are mediums." The difference between the two arises from the distinct level of consciousness the intuitive person is attuning to as well as the style of discernment they are using.

A psychic discerns information about incarnated humans. In other words, the psychic and their client are both in physical form. Therefore, psychic details come from the energy-information field of the physical dimension. The information shared can pertain to current issues or it can involve predictions about the future.

Mediums attune to the higher selves of souls that are no longer in a body. Unlike psychic work, in which the intuitive discerns data from a person's energy field, mediums engage spirits in real-time, two-way communication.

It may be helpful to think of the different levels or expressions of consciousness like musical octaves. Spirit represents all the possible notes, but its music is expressed in groupings with differing but relational vibrations.

The dimension we find ourselves in after a physical incarnation is often referred to as the astral realm. This is analogous to the next higher octave on the spectrum of consciousness. Angels exist and work in the next higher octave after the astral; archangels in the next one up; and so forth, with Spirit representing the entire symphony of LIFE.

Our earthly, incarnated experiences take place in an octave of tones that is lower or denser than the higher realms. Psychics tune in only to this octave. Mediums attune to the higher octaves, but since they are immersed in the vibrations of the earthly realm, it is quite easy to also tune in psychically.

Attuning to the higher octaves is simply a refinement of the same discernment skills a psychic uses. Because we are all souls, there is no reason psychics—and you—cannot learn to attune to the higher realms.

It is not unusual during a mediumistic session for a medium to *go psychic* and tune into the energy-information field of their client. Unlike a psychic, however, some of the information can also come by interacting with the client's guides at the higher octaves. While this can be informative and often fun, a medium's principal goal is to connect with those who have passed to provide healing and comfort, as well as to show the continuity of consciousness.

# TYPES OF MEDIUMSHIP

When you want to connect long-distance with a loved one here in the earthly realm, you have a variety of choices. You can pick up the phone and chat, you can do a video conference call, email them, or even write a letter. All methods allow you to communicate your thoughts and feelings, but each has its unique limitations and benefits. Which one you choose depends upon your skill with the modality and how convenient and timely it is.

The same is true with mediumship. Each style which follows allows a medium to communicate with those in the spirit world, with varying limitations.

## MENTAL MEDIUMSHIP

This method is the most well-known because it is the most common. It is also the style featured most in the media and public events. A mental medium can do private sessions for one person or conduct demonstrations of mediumship, also known as gallery readings, for groups of varying sizes. In mental mediumship, communication takes place and is interpreted through the mind or consciousness of the medium.

## PHYSICAL MEDIUMSHIP

This type of communication occurs when those in the spirit world manipulate the physical world to reveal their presence. Physical mediumship is rare today. It was much more common in the twentieth century, when mediums, undistracted by modern technology, took the time to sit regularly in small groups to focus their energy on higher octaves of consciousness. Those in spirit then use the higher vibrations produced by these dedicated mediums to produce phenomena that are visible or audible to all present.

While physical mediumship clearly demonstrates the presence of spirit beings, it does not always provide the frequency and clarity of messages as mental mediumship. The Fox Sisters' story of discerning rapping from across the veil is an excellent example of physical mediumship with accompanying messages. The most important message, however, is "We are here!" This can become quite clear when those in spirit allow physical objects to appear seemingly out of thin air.

I had the honor of writing Mavis Pittilla's biography, and it was thrilling to listen to her recount stories of sitting weekly with a circle of other mediums for the purpose of physical mediumship. They sang songs and used their intention to raise the energy and build their power.

These dedicated mediums would often sit for weeks with no results, but their efforts paid off. Mavis told stories of her chair levitating to the ceiling while she sat in it, of metal trumpets flying around the room, and of a carrot materializing up through the floor in view of all. Such experiences may be difficult to believe, but I know and trust Mavis. Her stories and those of others attest to this most wondrous way that those in spirit show their presence.

## CHANNELING

As the word implies, a medium serves as the intermediary or channel between those in the physical world and those in spirit. In gallery readings and one-on-one sessions, the medium passes along the evidence and messages in a third person ("he said" or "she said") manner while in a fully conscious state. Some people use the word *channeling* to describe this process, but in traditional terms, channeling occurs when the medium enters a deeper state of consciousness and allows those in spirit to speak directly through them in first-person terms, using the pronoun I. In this beautiful method of blending with the spirit, the medium might take on the mannerisms, gestures, facial expressions, word choice, and accent of the person they are channeling.

This type of mediumship is often called *trance channeling*. It's important to understand that true trance, in which the medium is completely unaware of what they are saying or doing, is rare. Edgar Cayce, known as The Sleeping Prophet, is an excellent example of someone who mastered trance and used it to provide information and healing for tens of thousands of people. The majority of those who channel today do so with varying degrees of awareness of what is being said. The goal of a channel, no matter whether in full or partial trance, is to allow spirits to speak freely without filtering the messages.

I have been channeling my guides, Sanaya, since 2010. While in this blended state, I am what is called a conscious channel rather than a trance channel. I am aware of the words I say, and I am listening and learning at the same time as others in the audience. To hear the words of Sanaya as they come through—to sit in the presence of that refined spirit energy—is a palpable experience of higher vibration ... of love. To hear their messages and be touched by their love is an experience that many present will never forget.

## AUTOMATIC WRITING

This solitary type of mediumship consists of sitting with the purpose of communing with those in spirit and writing the words and wisdom that arise as a result. In true automatic writing, the spirits control the medium's hand and pen. Like physical mediumship, this is rare. More commonly, the medium listens and writes the inspirations and messages from spirit, much like taking dictation.

Automatic writing is an excellent way to carry on a conversation with a loved one who has passed. It is thus highly useful for personal communications across the veil, whether you are a professional medium or not. I have received downloads from Sanaya daily since 2010, amassing thousands of inspirational messages. While the insights they share are universal, I often use automatic writing to record responses to my own questions that come through in this effective mode of spirit communication.

Setting aside time to enter a more expanded state of consciousness and commune with a spirit person helps to hold the focus more clearly, resulting in conversations that are often helpful and healing. The words that flow come with an awareness that the receiver is not making up what is often called a download from spirit. It can be utterly transformational to have the firsthand experience that support and love are always as close as our breath.

# HEALING FROM A
# HIGHER PERSPECTIVE

odern media and television programs that feature mediums have helped bring the subject to a mainstream audience. Still, mediumship remains mysterious to many and is too often relegated to the category of entertainment.

Some may consult a medium for the fun of it. There is no doubt that it tickles our human fancy to have a stranger reveal surprising and astounding details from the spirit world that they have no way of knowing. I hope I never lose the awe of passing along a message or detail that makes my clients gasp and their eyes widen like saucers.

But mediumship is far more than the stuff of movies. Often, grief is the main reason a person seeks a reading. Those who are fearful about speaking to spirits and those who may have never given much thought to the afterlife will often overcome their hesitation to sit with a medium after the death of a close family member, friend, or beloved animal companion.

Faced with the unacceptable and incorrect belief that they will never see their loved one again, people from all walks of life are more willing to set their doubts aside. Once they do, the results of a clear and verifiable connection are often transformational.

In the previous chapter, you learned that one of the main goals of mediumship is to prove the continuity of consciousness and provide healing and comfort on multiple levels: mental, emotional, spiritual, and even physical. This is because mediumship allows those on both sides of the veil to address past as well as current issues.

## DEALING WITH THE PAST

We are all painfully aware that we and those we love could be gone in an instant—yet we hesitate to talk openly about death. As a self-protective measure, we relegate thoughts of our ultimate demise to the back of our mind. Nevertheless, death is never far away; awareness of the fragility of our bodies hangs like the sword of Damocles over our heads.

As a result, most people put off important conversations about death, feeling those discussions can wait until later. This can cause serious challenges when there is a sudden or unexpected death.

A good medium is aware of the healing potential of mediumship. They will remain watchful for messages from the spirit world that address things left unsaid between the spirit and their client. While some spirit messages such as "It's beautiful here," are impossible to validate, many healing messages prove their authenticity when they include issues about which the medium is unaware.

Some of the most evidential and healing messages include expressions of gratitude from across the veil. Some of those who were ill before passing wish to thank their loved one for their end-of-life care. Spirits may also validate that decisions made on their behalf were good ones, thus alleviating a burden by those who wonder if they did the right thing for their loved one in their final days and hours.

Other expressions of gratitude include thank you's for special memories or gifts exchanged. Of these gifts, the greatest, of course, is the love shared between two people. For this reason, messages of gratitude are frequently accompanied by an apology for not expressing one's love more openly or more often, or for neglecting to express it at all. Those on both sides of the veil often wish to apologize for times when they were less than loving. When the connection is clear, the exact details surrounding these circumstances come through from those in spirit. Such issues can range from minor tiffs to major abuse and neglect.

## LIFE IN REVIEW

When people pass to the other side, most go through a life review. With spirit guides at their side, they view their entire life as if it is a movie playing out in fast motion. But unlike in a movie, they also see the effects of each action they took, no matter how small. They feel the actual reactions and emotions of everyone their choices affected.

With the higher perspective afforded by no longer being in a body, many spirits now want to apologize for specific incidents and behaviors. Mediumship allows them to do so.

I often have spirits tell me, "My eyes have been opened here!" By this, they mean that they now understand that the most important thing we come into physical form to do is to love each other fully. Once the body no longer blocks our awareness of our true nature, we feel the unconditional love that surrounds us. Having instantly felt the love and learned this important lesson, those across the veil are grateful for the opportunity to express their love as fully as possible.

Some people might not wish to hear from a loved one who hurt them in some way. But when they understand that the spirits have come to make amends, tremendous healing can take place in a safe, compassionate, and loving atmosphere.

Until we realize that we are souls here and now, our human egos cause us to behave in ways that are often judgmental and rigid. We hold onto constricting and painful beliefs. Because of the higher perspective afforded in the afterlife, those in the spirit world often want to ask for or offer forgiveness. Mediumship provides the opportunity for those on both sides of the veil to do so.

I once brought through a client's mother who appeared in my mind's eye with her head bowed. I recognized this symbol of an apology and reported it to my client. Hearing this, the woman immediately stiffened, so I silently asked her mother in spirit for details. When I explained that her mother wanted to apologize for abandoning her as a baby—a fact I did not know— my client replied with great bitterness, "That's right. She abandoned me and my eight brothers and sisters."

The mother then filled my mind with images and emotions that made it clear why she had made the decision to leave her family. As the information flowed, my client looked stunned and visibly let down her guard. At the end of the session, when she got up to leave, she turned to me and said, "I've carried around anger at my mother for seventy-five years, and in less than an hour, it's gone."

This is a remarkable yet common example of the healing power of mediumship. It also shows the value of shifting your perspective now and viewing your current and past relationships from the soul's point of view. In other words, don't wait until you require a medium to give thanks and make amends.

Forgiveness results when you come to understand that hurt people hurt people. Forgiveness doesn't condone hurtful acts; it acknowledges that people make mistakes and do painful things to others when they forget we are souls. Forgiveness is a gift you give yourself. It sets you free from the bonds that are holding you captive to past events and people.

Thanks to mediumship, it is never too late to make amends.

# SUICIDE AND OVERDOSE

Spirits who passed by suicide, overdose, or by any means for which they take responsibility are usually eager to apologize for the pain their passing has caused to those still in physical form. They also want their loved ones to know that they are surrounded by love and they are healing.

The idea that those who pass as a result of suicide are sent to a hellish place is promoted by many religions, but it is not supported by mediumship. Those who crossed over before completing what could have been a lengthier time on Earth report that the challenging circumstances they underwent while in physical form are accepted and understood. They are shown how they might have made better choices, and they're given the opportunity to continue growing and serving—from the spirit world.

# EVIDENCE THAT SHOWS ONGOING PRESENCE

After the death of a loved one, it is natural to lament the things we think they will miss. Mediumship dispels such false thinking. Those in the spirit world tell us that they can be in multiple places at once and look in on those they care about. They claim they are more present in their family's and friends' lives after they pass than before. Thanks to occupying a realm without time or space, they merely need to think of someone, and they are instantly in their presence.

It can be immensely comforting to know that those in spirit are still part of our lives. Loved ones across the veil often talk about their funerals, showing that they heard the music or saw items that were put in the coffin with them. They also acknowledge births in the family and loved ones who have graduated, gotten married or divorced, acquired a new job, sold a house, and other major life events.

What a comfort it is to know that special occasions bring our loved ones in spirit even closer!

## ADDRESSING CURRENT ISSUES

Those in spirit will often comment during a reading about current issues in their loved ones' lives. These can be simple, everyday things such as describing what a loved one ate for breakfast or a specific item they just bought.

I once had a mother in spirit show me a lily in a small pot that my client—her daughter—had just received. My client denied any knowledge of this plant, despite my clear description of it. Five minutes after the phone reading concluded, the client called me back to share her excitement. Her doorbell had rung in the middle of our session, but she ignored it so as not to interrupt the connection with her mother.

When my client opened the door after the reading concluded, she found on the porch an unexpected delivery from a local florist. It was a potted white lily, exactly as her mother had described it. Her mom had the bird's-eye view while she visited with both of us.

Spirits also show—often to the surprise or chagrin of the message recipient—that they know about family disputes and poor behavior. In these cases, there is no judgment from across the veil. Instead, those in spirit offer helpful advice, if doing so won't interfere with a life lesson that the person here needs to learn.

One mother in spirit asked me to tell her adult daughter, "If I had known what that money would do to the family, I would have burned it before I left." My wide-eyed client confirmed that her siblings were embroiled in a lawsuit over their mother's estate.

Because they are now able to sense our feelings and hear our thoughts, those across the veil do their best to encourage and guide us in our day-to-day lives. I have had spirits lovingly convey such evidential messages as, "You need to stop drinking so much," "You need to get out of bed and get more fresh air," or "It's okay to be happy. There's no need to cry so much about me. I'm right here with you."

In giving advice, some spouses in spirit let their bereaved partners know that it's okay to find love again when the time is right. There are also those in spirit who validate the fact that they enjoyed a true soul-mate relationship with their partner and acknowledge that the surviving partner might never again be interested in another relationship. Mediumship mirrors life in that way: every connection, just like every relationship, is unique.

## ANIMALS IN THE AFTERLIFE

The soul is the vital aspect that enlivens the body and continues after death as a unique field of energy-information. It stands to reason—and mediumship provides the validation—that animals are souls in physical form.

Just as there is an energy field unique to the human species, each animal species has what could be termed a "group soul." If there are identifying features or a particular story associated with a specific animal, a medium can attune to the soul or energy field of that animal and communicate with it individually after it leaves its physical form.

Animals who served as human companions during their lifetime have unique personalities and character traits that distinguish their energy field from the group soul of their species. This makes it possible for mediums to connect heart-to-heart with these beloved creatures who maintain ties with their human family members from across the veil.

I have connected with many cats and dogs and even a horse who provided meaningful memories and messages that left no doubt in my client's mind that we were connecting with their animal companions. Because communication takes place from a level beyond the physical senses, the information exchanged is translated by the medium's brain into words and images.

Just like communicating with humans, the most common messages from animal companions across the veil are expressions of love and gratitude.

# THE RESPONSIBILITY OF MEDIUMSHIP

I will never forget a client whose doctor sent her to me as a last resort to heal her deep depression. I knew nothing about why she sought a medium, but it became clear when I tuned in and sensed her husband across the veil.

Among other things, the man in spirit wanted me to tell his wife how pleased he was that she was planning to travel for the first time since he died of a sudden heart attack. He showed me that she had purchased a ticket to fly to England with a friend.

The woman gaped at me and asked, "How do you know all that?" I replied that her husband was right there in the room with us and was telling me this information.

As if to prove this point, the husband then said very clearly, "Please tell my wife, don't you dare take those pills in your purse!" I repeated his words verbatim and watched my client's eyes widen even more.

"Nobody knows this," she said, "but I stopped at the drug store on the way here, and I bought enough pills to do myself in if I didn't hear from my husband."

This stunning example demonstrates the great responsibility mediums carry. I ran into this woman a year later and was thrilled to see her smiling and living her life fully once again. I am forever grateful to the woman's doctor, her husband, and the other unseen helpers in spirit who brought us together at just the right time.

Due to the nature of their work, mediums regularly deal with people in deep grief, many of whom have unresolved issues. It is not a medium's job to be a therapist, but it is critical that the medium represents the thoughts and desires of those in spirit accurately.

My friend and colleague, Mavis Pittilla, one of the great British mediums of all time and an incomparable teacher of mediumship, taught her students the importance of being the clearest possible voice for those in the spirit world. She stated —only half-jokingly— "You don't want to cross the veil and have a spirit say, 'I never said those things that you told my loved one!'"

For this reason, I consider "Do no harm" to be rule number one in mediumship. Within seconds or minutes, a medium can be privy to some of the most private and intimate issues in a person's life. We discern things that some people would never tell a soul. This is possible because we are communicating soul to soul.

It might appear that a medium serves as a therapist, but this is not the case. A medium is simply the intermediary. They serve as the mouthpiece for those in spirit, not a counselor. Healing often occurs quite naturally when the two worlds unite and those on both sides of the veil can clear the air.

A mediumship reading can be deeply healing and comforting, helping not only with grief, but aiding in the resolution of unfinished concerns of a lifetime. If you have a message for someone who has passed, know that you don't need a medium to share with them whatever is in your heart. Send your sentiments via your thoughts or say them aloud. It makes no difference to those in spirit. They hear you either way. With patience and practice you can get to the point where you discern and trust their response.

# ACROSS THE VEIL

*W*hen consulting a medium, it is helpful to clearly express your intention as to the type of reading you want. Some people who sit with a medium are more interested in connecting with guides and angels. Many mediums can and do connect with spirit guides and occasionally with their clients' animal companions across the veil. However, the goal of most traditionally trained mediums is to help their clients connect with their family members and friends who have passed.

It is possible to communicate with any soul at any level of reality because we are all multidimensional souls. This includes archangels and ascended masters. These beings operate on the higher octaves on the spectrum of consciousness than the astral realm, which is the principle focus of most mediums.

In the astral realm, in addition to family and friends, you might even encounter a cadre of formerly famous people from all walks of life who are using their celebrity status to help humanity. Whether or not a famous person you wish to reach responds to your intentions depends upon whether such communications will serve the greater good.

If you have a true need for advice or connection that will help you or others on our earthly journey, most higher beings across the veil will do their best to make their presence known. If, however, you are trying to impress others by connecting with a celebrity who has passed, your efforts may be in vain.

Certain spirits, including your own loved ones, may hold back if it is not the right time for you to hear from them. My stepdaughter only recently explained to me why it took almost three years of effort before I connected with her for the first time in meditation. She told me that had she made her presence known earlier, I would not have given as much attention to the specific practices that lead to the best mediumistic connections, including clearing my energy field, raising my consciousness, and learning to quiet and focus my mind.

You'll find more about this topic in Part 3.

## HOW IS THIS POSSIBLE?

I will never forget the day my mentor, the late Janet Nohavec, called me to the front of her class in evidential mediumship in Lily Dale, New York, and put me on the spot.

"Suzanne, there's a spirit here who belongs to someone in this room," she said. "I want you to see what you can discern."

Janet had hired me to write her biography. I was sitting in the back of the room solely to observe how she worked. I had no intention of becoming a medium—but Janet had other ideas.

My Navy training did not allow me to refuse her request. I wanted nothing more than to rush out the door as I stood in front of the students trying to answer Janet's questions as she asked: Is the spirit male or female? How did they pass? How old were they, and what kind of work did they do?

I felt as if I were pulling data from the air as I robotically replied that the spirit was male who passed at age 70 from cancer and worked as an engineer. No one was more surprised than me when a woman in the class raised her hand and said, "I think it is my father you are describing."

I might have chalked this up to coincidence, but Janet followed with details of her own about the woman's father. I could not deny that we were tuning into something, although I felt no physical presence.

"What else do you see?" Janet asked me.

"I am seeing an image of black, patent leather shoes. And I just heard the word, Twinkletoes."

The man's daughter smiled with delight. "My father was a ballroom dancer," she said, "and my mother always called him Twinkletoes!"

As I will further detail in Part 3, from that moment forward, I dedicated myself to learning how this connection is possible and improving my ability to discern accurate information and messages. I set out to learn all I could about the nature of reality. I focused on ancient spiritual wisdom as well as the latest research in consciousness and quantum physics. This crucial process of *educating myself* turned out to be the first "E" in what I now call "The Three Es" of living The Awakened Way®.

At the same time that I was diving into books and learning more from Janet, my meditative practice opened me to the second "E": *Experience expanded reality for yourself.* I began to make personal contact with non-physical beings on a regular basis while in expanded states of consciousness. As I did so, I followed through with the third "E" by *engaging* each being, to learn from them as much as I could about the greater reality.

As you employ The Three E's, you will learn that things are not always what they seem. You will come to see that your bodily senses can easily deceive you into thinking that what you perceive through your eyes, ears, and sense of touch, taste, and smell is the one and only reality. This limited viewpoint can keep you from using your non-physical senses to perceive the multidimensional universe and tap into its riches.

As I pursued my own education process, I came to understand that the brain is not the source of consciousness. It is, instead, a beautifully designed instrument that functions as a receiver and a transmitter. The brain receives energy-information that flows within the one mind of Spirit that all beings share. It then translates each unique energetic signal into experiences that make sense to our human minds.

As one of its many functions, the brain acts as a filter of consciousness. This is a blessing. Without this filtering process, you would experience chaos. Just imagine if you were aware of all the cell phone, television, and radio signals being transmitted around you right now. You would not be able to function due to information overload.

The problem is that the brain also filters out the frequency bands of the higher realms. Non-physical beings are around you now, sharing information within the vast sea of consciousness, but your brain excludes these signals. The good news is that you can learn to bypass the filters so that you can tap into the higher realms on a limited basis.

## WHERE IS THE SPIRIT WORLD?

We speak of going to heaven when we die. What and where is heaven? By *Educating* yourself, *Experiencing* the spirit world for yourself, and *Engaging* spirits for yourself you will come to see that heaven is a state of consciousness that is here, wherever you are. Heaven is available to you right now and always.

You will understand, therefore, that when you cross the veil, you do not go to a far-off place. You exist in the eternal here-and-now as a beautiful expression of the one Source.

To explain how everything can be right here, despite our inability to sense alternate realities objectively, allow me to use the analogy of a television. Say you turn on a TV and watch a movie with your favorite actors. Are the characters they portray inside the television? Of course not. The television is simply an instrument that is perfectly designed to attune to a certain bandwidth of signals that are present and project them onto its screen as images and sounds that are meaningful to you.

So, what happens if a television mounted on the wall falls off and breaks? It can no longer display anything intelligible. But where did the signals that were previously visible and audible go? The answer is obvious: The signals didn't go anywhere. They are still here broadcasting, even when there is nothing to receive and translate those signals.

The physical body is analogous to the TV set. The body is an instrument that displays your unique story and character. The character you portray is not in your body. Your story is the projection of energy-information—signals—from within the mind of your soul, which is a projection of the one mind of Source.

So, what happens if, like the TV set, your body or the body of someone you love breaks and can no longer display your souls' signal? Where does the signal go?

Hopefully, you can now see that your signal—what we call the soul—doesn't go anywhere. It is still here, arising as an individuated, eternal, unique, and deeply beloved projection of Source.

The brain is the transceiver within the television set that is your body. It is perfectly tuned for the bandwidth of energy-information of this earthly realm. It is not so perfectly tuned, however, for picking up and properly displaying the signals of the higher realms. In fact, it filters out far more signals than it detects.

While it may sound impersonal and mechanistic to refer to loved ones as "signals of energy-information," it is the spirit within that gives life to all beings. This spark of the Divine is the basic essence of LIFE (Love In Full Expression).

Mediums have learned to bypass the brain's filters and access higher frequencies. They perceive these frequencies as the sensations, thoughts, and feelings of unique beings who exist beyond our realm of space and time.

Those in spirit are not far away, and it does not take time for them to come to you when they wish to communicate. Their signals, just like yours, are here, now, ever-present.

All of this explains what my friend Brenda meant when she came to me within hours of crossing the veil and said, "I'm right here, Suzanne! There's only here!"

Brenda is correct: There is nowhere to go when we die—we simply change states of consciousness.

Just as we humans are unique patterns of energy-information, so are the objects around us and the earthly realm as a whole. With this understanding, we can expand our analogy of eddies in the sea of consciousness. Each dimension is also a whirlpool within the wholeness. The astral realm, or what many call heaven, is not far away, but a reality that interpenetrates our own, albeit at a different frequency.

There is only here. The consciousness that perceives this current reality, right here and now, is the same consciousness that perceives all realities. What changes is the patterns of sensations, thoughts, and feelings that arise within this consciousness. We call these patterns of ST-F "experience."

Through mediumship, one learns to experience sensations, thoughts, and feelings in multiple realities by setting aside the normal human modes of perception. There is no need to go anywhere to do this, because the spirit world is right here.

# WHAT THE AFTERLIFE IS LIKE

Six weeks before my stepdaughter passed, I found a book about the afterlife by medium James van Praagh. I had no idea that my life was about to change in unimaginable ways nor that I would become a colleague and friend of James. I bought his book out of curiosity, but initially I couldn't bring myself to believe the things he claimed our loved ones are doing in the afterlife.

According to James, spirit people are living in houses, working in jobs, and participating in an assortment of other activities that sound very much like those we partake in here in the physical world.

I can tell you now that those in spirit construct houses, albeit using the mind, much like you might build structures in your dreams. They also work and participate in fun activities on the other side of the veil! I say this thanks to the preponderance of stories backed up by verifiable evidence that those in spirit have shared with me firsthand after I developed my abilities as a medium.

We can't prove what the afterlife is like, but the evidence-based stories bring us as close to proof as we can hope for until we experience it for ourselves. My favorite example of one such story occurred when I did a session for a woman whose husband had passed. I validated his presence by correctly describing his personality, detailing his cause of death, the kind of work he did, and sharing other identifying details.

After passing along the man's heartfelt messages for his wife, she asked me if he could tell us what he was doing on the other side. I asked the question and laughed aloud.

"He says, 'I'm standing firmly on two feet and playing golf every day.'"

Even though I was aware by that time that heaven is much more like James van Praagh's description than the limited version I'd previously believed, I still felt a bit silly passing along what seemed like a fanciful reply.

The man's wife, however, seemed quite pleased to hear this news. She explained to me that golf was her husband's passion—a bit of evidence that she had not yet shared.

What she told me next gave even more credence to his response. Unbeknownst to me, her husband's leg had been amputated and he was unable to golf in his final years. No wonder he was eager to let her know he was "standing firmly on two feet" and playing his favorite sport!

In addition to hearing stories like these from those across the veil, my guides gifted me some years back with a lengthy description of what the afterlife is like. This came as a long download in response to a question from Dr. Kenneth Ring, one of the world's foremost experts on near-death experiences (NDEs). When I delivered the guides' discourse to Dr. Ring, a psychologist who has interviewed and reported the accounts of thousands of people who have had an NDE, he stated, "I don't think I have ever read a more astonishing document addressed to me in my life. I am somewhere between awe and amazed."

The following is an excerpt from that incredibly special download—direct from the spirit world—to help you understand from the spirit world's perspective what the afterlife is like.

> As to the so-called "other side," it is not a place, but a state of consciousness. What place are you in each night as you dream? Can you pinpoint it on your map? Yet it is very real to you, is it not? The experiences you have in your dreams are very real, very solid. You move about as you do in human form, yet lo! Suddenly you are flying.
>
> This is true freedom in the next world. There is no sense of pain. There is no hunger. Yet, there are emotions. There is a bit of fright at times, as well as moments of sheer bliss. Welcome to the first level of consciousness after passing ... but only—

and this is quite important—if you have passed to the other side having achieved a level of consciousness that is relative to the mass of human consciousness.

In other words, most of your fellow human beings who have not done much homework in the arena of raising their consciousness will find themselves in this dreamlike place/ state of walking, flying, eating, singing, studying, playing golf, living in houses, playing a musical instrument, and all those other so-called human activities which you enjoy now.

That word "enjoy" is quite important. "Why would you eat on the other side?" you ask, and we wish to tell you that it is not for nutrition, but for the sheer enjoyment of it. Would it not be "heaven" to be able to eat ten of your berry pies and not blow up like a big, fat berry yourself?

If you always wanted to sky dive, and you arrive on the other side at the first level of graduation consciousness, why then, you sky dive at will. The airplane magically appears, and perhaps it is flown by your best friend from high school who always wanted to be a pilot. And when the time comes to jump out of the plane, why, you don't even need a parachute and you feel no fear. It is quite a thrill, and you realize, "I am creating this! I am controlling this dream!"

And therein lies the key. The more of these realizations you have that you are creating your experiences, and that creation is instantaneous, the less you need to hold onto this lower level of human-like consciousness. Your parachute disappears first, and then your flight suit, and you find yourself naked, and do you know what? You are not embarrassed, for you realize, "Wait a moment! This body is no more real than my parachute! I no more need this body than I need a parachute!"

But you still wish to have form, and so you now don a white robe. Or perhaps you have always liked purple. It matters not. The meaningful point here is that you have just moved up a notch and no longer need your "human suit." You have now graduated to the next level up on the ladder of consciousness. You dress in robes, but only if your consciousness wishes to differentiate yourself from the others you now find about you in robes.

And what are you doing there "all day" in this environment in which the sun never sets, yet in which there is no sun but simply an ever-present warm glow that you feel as much as you see? You and your robed friends no longer eat, for you have finally satisfied those human desires for simple pleasures and instant gratification. You have now realized that gratification is the result of simply knowing who you are.

You now know who you are: A being in a state of being, and you experience gratitude and the awareness that you are love. You now want nothing more than to share that love with others and to help them rise to the level you have achieved. You realize that this is what it is all about—this experience of differentiated consciousness.

You realize that you have arisen from the sea of undifferentiated consciousness, but you are not yet ready to return fully to that state. You have work to do.

You now take on a mission of a higher kind. You become a spirit guide to others, or perhaps you help those who have recently passed over, or perhaps you minister to those who have taken their own lives.

You may help those who find themselves at the sub-levels of human consciousness—those who never did fully grasp the *concept of love whilst in human form and perpetuated acts of so-called evil. They are not left to feel their remorse alone. You may decide to stand silently at their side to let them know that when they are ready to face their actions they will be guided gently and lovingly to a higher level.*

*And as you do this work you are rewarded, for the same law that is in effect at the human level comes into play: You reap what you sow. You have now done a tour of duty in this level. You make a choice as to how you can benefit the whole in the greatest capacity. As your learning increases and your growth increases along with it, you are rewarded by your own actions, and you move up the ladder, as it were.*

*Now you no longer need a robe. Now you are pure light. Now you circulate more freely amongst those at the other levels. Those with eyes to see will see your glow. Your fellow lights know you by the particular glow or vibration of your light, and so, you see, you have no need for names or clothes.*

*What do you do all day? You are. You love. By your very presence you raise the consciousness of the whole. You teach. You glow. You need not do anything. Your environment is not an environment. You no longer have a need for houses, or schools, or music, or things. Your music is the vibration of love. It is all around you and you know it as you.*

*Yet still, you know there is more. There is the entirety of all that is you.*

*Now, we wish to explain that one does not necessarily rise through the ranks, as it were, in a linear fashion. Life is like a spiral. Growth occurs in this spiral fashion. You are not actually slipping backwards should you decide to have another go at it as a human, for you will return to human form vibrating at a higher level and taking back with you more love than the last time you incarnated.*

*And so it is when you leave. Over and over, you may return to that state of consciousness immediately following loss of the human body where there is form, and structure, and clothing, and berry pies, until one day you have risen high enough on the spiral that you decide you are ready to take it to the next level.*

*And that is how it goes ... spiraling, spiraling at the exact pace that is right for your soul.*

*There is no competition with other souls. There is no race. There is no judgment or comparison. There is blending, however ... blending of soul energy the higher you go. That state of perfect blending with All That Is lies within all of you always. It is the recognition of this, your Source, your Essence, which keeps you—all of you—moving ever onward and upward along the spiral.*

*And so, consciousness creates your reality. What is your state of consciousness now? That will be your reality the moment you pass to the other side. Do you have attachments to food and music and things and people? Then you will need to surround yourself with those things when you get to the other side, and so it will be. Do you expect nothing but darkness? Then that will be your experience, but only for a brief time, until one of the beings of light standing at your side helps you to open your eyes and see the light.*

*Have you achieved the state of consciousness where you realize now that you could live very well without food and music and things, but you very much appreciate them? Do you realize now that you are the love you seek? Do you want nothing more than to help your fellow man?*

*Do you feel compassion and understanding for all your fellow beings, no matter their transgressions in this lifetime? Why then, our friend, we daresay you will jump to the head of the class, catapulting right over the heads of those souls sitting in classrooms on the other side, right past those falling out of perfectly good spirit airplanes, and right past the bakery display cases, to live amongst the robed beings.*

*You create your own reality ... here, now, and in every now-moment that follows, for now is all there is. The levels of the afterlife are not clearly delineated as many would desire. We will not number them or label them precisely, although we have attempted to do so somewhat with a bit of humor to satisfy your human curiosity and desires to stratify, and quantify, and qualify.*

*These different experiences are simply notes on a scale rising ever higher ... different tones of vibration with specific experiences pertaining to each note. What song are you singing now? That will be the song you hear when you pass from your physical body.*

# REINCARNATION

The guides spoke above about the choice to enter back into physical human form and have another go at it. As a medium, I speak to many still here in a body who have endured the kind of trauma and tragedy that leads them to state emphatically, "I am never coming back!"

This attitude is understandable when one views human suffering in the context of a single lifetime. Reincarnation, however, provides purpose and meaning to the challenges we face in our earthly lives by showing that every experience and every lifetime is part of the cycles and processes within the ongoing experiences of the soul.

Reincarnation is not just a concept or a theory. The fact that we have experienced human life in a body before and will incarnate again has been validated by the work of respected researchers, with one of the most thorough collections of examples compiled by Dr. Ian Stevenson at the University of Virginia.

Dr. Stevenson and his colleagues interviewed thousands of children who remember vivid details of past lives that can be verified. Many of these children have birthmarks related to the way the person they identify as their previous incarnation passed. A large group of them were able to identify the houses where they had lived in previous lives while also knowing the names and relationships of relatives from the life before.

Beyond academicians, mediums also attest to the validity of reincarnation by tapping into past life evidence of both their clients and those across the veil. The information gleaned can prove helpful in identifying the cause of current personality traits and propensities, phobias, fears, and relationship challenges of which the medium was unaware.

One of the most common questions my clients and students ask me is, "What happens if my loved one reincarnates before I cross the veil?" I assure them—and you—that there is no need to worry.

The soul is a microcosm of the macrocosm of Consciousness. Just as limitless whirlpools arise from and within the one sea of consciousness, so, too, is the soul so much more than the limited expression of a single lifetime. The soul can and does produce countless swirling creations we call lifetimes. The recognizable pattern that you identify as yourself or your loved one remains a part of the larger eddy of the soul forever.

From a mediumistic point of view, I was especially fascinated by the story of a young boy told in the book *Soul Survivor* by Bruce and Andrea

Leininger. The evidence is clear that this boy is the reincarnation of a U.S. Navy pilot who died when his combat aircraft crashed in World War II. At one point in the book, the boy's father took him to a reunion of the pilot's squadron mates.

Having never met any of these men and without knowing their stories, the boy approached several of them and identified them by name. Just as you would know an old friend if you heard their voice at a party decades later, this boy recognized their voices across lifetimes.

In one especially poignant moment, the boy had the chance to visit his sister from his lifetime as the military pilot. He recognized her home as if it had been his home, for in another lifetime, it had been! He accurately described how his bedroom was decorated in the pre-war era, including the pilot's personal items and where they were placed.

When I read this part of the book, I understood the deeper dynamics from a medium's perspective. I knew that if the pilot's sister, in her eighties when the young boy visited, had asked a medium to connect with her long-deceased brother, the medium would have been able to do so. It would make no difference that the same soul was now experiencing life as this young boy.

Do not make the very human mistake of seeing the soul/human relationship as a one-to-one, all-or-nothing relationship. Human beings do not dissolve into nothingness when the physical lifetime ends. The soul is far greater than one character with one story.

The Story of You does not end at death, even if the soul makes the conscious choice to spin a new story of itself like a whirlpool into another lifetime for a fresh adventure in consciousness.

Each lifetime is part of the wholeness of the soul, and the soul is much greater than the sum of its parts. With education, intention, and commitment, it is well within the capacity of each one of us to open ourselves to the higher vibratory realms of Spirit. We can then begin to experience a new and rewarding connection with loved ones, guides, angels, and ascended masters.

# MAKING THE CONNECTION

ediumship is two-way communication with those in the non-physical realms. At its core, communication is the exchange of information. With this understanding, you can see that it is not necessary for those in spirit to speak to us. Spoken communication is only one way that non-physical beings can share news, notifications, knowledge, emotions, and meaningful messages.

Some people have seen and sensed spirits since childhood. They have no doubt that the spirit world is real, and they interact with higher beings as naturally as they do in their physical relationships. But for most humans, mediumship opens you to another world.

If you were going to travel to a foreign country, you might pick up a book or consult the internet to understand the cultural rules and the best ways of communicating. It's the same with mediumship. Consider this your guide to the spirit world.

# HOW THOSE IN SPIRIT COMMUNICATE WITH US

Beings in spirit make their presence known via direct, two-way communication as well as through indirect experiences. Both methods are considered ADCs and are often spontaneous and can occur to anyone at any time.

Mediumship takes ADCs to a higher level by communicating willingly with intention. A clear connection is much more likely when this intention is grounded in love and based on a desire to serve the greatest possible good.

A medium can communicate with those in spirit directly, using both non-physical and physical senses. Traditionally, these senses are categorized into what are known in mediumship as "the clairs." The prefix comes from the French word for clear, which is always the goal when interacting with those in the non-physical realms. The following are the main methods of direct spirit communication.

## CLAIRVOYANCE

Many people use this term to describe reading the future, although the correct term for making psychic predictions is *prophecy*. The true meaning of *clairvoyance* is "clear seeing." This sense can refer to both prophecy and discerning information from the spirit world in the form of images or visions. If a person sees an object or a person outside of them with their eyes open, this is called *objective clairvoyance*.

Most commonly, imagery appears to mediums in what is known as the "mind's eye" or on "the screen of the mind." This skill is called *subjective clairvoyance*. It can occur with eyes open or closed. To experience how this works, hold out your hand and picture an apple in it. You can discern details such as the color and size, and it doesn't matter if your eyes are open or not. Your mind is projecting the image. That is exactly what those in spirit do. They project what they want you to see as an image that arises in your awareness.

Those in spirit will take advantage of the adage, "A picture is worth a thousand words." With a single, evocative image they can communicate a message that goes straight to the heart. Their most important message might be, "I'm still right here." This truth can be validated with clairvoyance.

One of my favorite examples occurred when a young man in spirit showed me a toothpick hanging out of his mouth. His mother shouted, "That's him! Everyone knows he was always chewing on a toothpick!"

That one image proved so profoundly meaningful to this grieving mother that her family and coworkers noticed the immediate lift in her mood. She weaned herself off antidepressants with the awareness that her toothpick-chewing son was supporting her from across the veil.

## CLAIRAUDIENCE

One of the most common ways we communicate with each other in this physical world is via the spoken word. With *clairaudience*, words arise from those in spirit as thoughts in the mind. This is known as *subjective clairaudience*. In rare cases, the spoken words of spirit are heard as if outside us in what is called *objective clairaudience*.

Mediums can hear words, phrases, song lyrics, music, and anything else we might normally sense auditorily. Ideally, we can engage in full conversations that leave no doubt that the exchange is taking place with a sentient, living being.

I experience clever, creative dialogues with spirits who speak in the same terms as when they used a physical voice. When a father in spirit had me tell his daughter, "I was a real son-of-a-gun," she knew the apology that followed came directly from him. I especially celebrate the session in which a daughter in spirit used my clairaudience to tell her father, "I love you to the moon and back." The words visibly startled him, for this was a phrase they often said to each other. They said it so often, in fact, that he wrote those exact words on her coffin.

## CLAIRSENTIENCE

Have you ever sensed that someone was standing behind you or watching you from across a room? Whether or not a person near you is in physical form or pure spirit, the faculty that allows you to sense their presence is *clairsentience.* The term means "clear feeling" and it applies to communication through sensation or emotion. For example, through clairsentience, spirits can communicate their emotions as well as personality and character traits that help loved ones to recognize and identify them.

Clairsentience also allows those in spirit to produce what feel like physical sensations in our human body to communicate a particular message. One doesn't need to be a medium to experience an invisible hand touching an arm or a tickle in the hair. These sensations may come with the thought or image of a loved one and a knowing in the heart that they are near.

Those in spirit use my clairsentience to produce symptoms in my body related to the way they passed. I give them permission to do so because this mode of proving their presence is so evidential. My heart will palpitate if the spirit person passed from a heart issue. They will momentarily take my breath away if they had lung issues. I have even experienced pain in my left kidney from a dog who passed from kidney disease.

Is my kidney actually twinging? Is my heart beating fast, or am I simply having an experience in my mind of kidney pain or an arrhythmia? It is impossible to know because all reality boils down to experiences arising in awareness. A medium learns to attune to the experiences arising from the energy field of those in spirit.

## CLAIRCOGNIZANCE

There are many things in life that we learn from being taught by others. This does not mean that everything that people teach us is true. Does the sun really set? No. That is something we learn and agree to accept, even though it is not really what is happening when the sun appears to dip below the horizon.

*Claircognizance* is the sensing faculty that allows us to know things without being taught or previously having a personal experience. We know what love feels like and we learn to call this feeling love. We know when we are uncomfortable. We learn to label discomfort hot or cold or hungry and so forth.

Those in spirit can communicate many things without needing images, words, or sensations. We simply know what they are trying to get across. The awareness arises with a certainty that can't be denied.

You may have felt a sudden, unwavering *knowing* that your loved one who has passed is nearby and aware of your life. This is claircognizance.

Ideally, each of the other clairs are combined with claircognizance when those in spirit communicate. A clear connection allows you to perceive claircognizantly that what you are seeing, hearing, and feeling is accurate.

## CLAIRGUSTANCE

Have you ever had an unexplained metallic taste in your mouth? This is an example of *clairgustance*. There was not actually a piece of metal in your mouth when this happened, but a specific frequency of energy-information was being communicated that the brain interpreted as "metallic taste in the mouth."

Unusual tastes can be messages from those in spirit. If your grandmother used to enjoy baking brownies and you suddenly experience the taste of those brownies when thinking about her, this is a wonderful way for her to let you know she is with you.

## CLAIRALIENCE

It's amazing how many things can be communicated through *clairalience*, or sensing smells. Those in spirit can create the frequency of a specific scent related to a meaningful object, memory, or event. This might be the scent of a favorite flower, a familiar perfume, a brand of pipe tobacco, and so forth.

Is the smoke from a pipe actually in the room when someone smells it, or is this a creative use of energy-information? Based on personal experience, it is the latter. I once did a reading despite having a cold. My nose was so blocked that I couldn't have smelled hot pizza if someone had put it directly in front of me.

During that reading, a father in spirit showed me a trunk of his that was in the attic of his daughter's home. I was able to describe the wartime photos and medals inside the trunk and clearly sensed a moldy, musty smell coming from it. My client had recently been looking through that very trunk and shared that she had noticed the musty smell I described.

What I sensed in that session using clairalience was indistinguishable from what the brain tells us is an actual moldy smell. This begs the question, what is real? As a wise guide in spirit once told me in meditation, *Anything that you can create in consciousness is real and can convey truth, messages, information, learning, healing, and growth.*

As you can see, the "clairs" allow us to interact with those in spirit using the equivalent of our physical senses. Any of the "clairs" may be stronger in one medium than another. Ideally, a medium naturally develops dexterity in each modality equally.

Likewise, each spirit may have a preferred way of communicating. If a person was particularly talkative when in physical form, once across the veil, they may utilize a medium's clairaudience in a reading. If one was visually creative and artistic, they might project more images, calling on the medium's clairvoyance.

Non-interactive contact from those in spirit occurs spontaneously to mediums and non-mediums alike. Those in spirit can see the human aura or energy field and can tell when their loved ones in physical form will be most likely to sense their presence. Ideal times for these connections are during meditation and when just falling asleep or awakening.

## THE DREAM STATE

We are also more open to contact during the dream state, when our attention is not so focused on the objective physical world. A dream visit from a loved one in spirit has quite a different feel from normal dreams. Those who enjoy these blessed experiences report a very real or solid quality to them. Unlike regular dreams that often fade away when we try to remember the details, dream visits stay with us. They are also always positive and love filled. Any dreams of loved ones that are fearful are not actual visits but a result of working through energy-information within the dreamer's subconscious mind.

## SIGNS AND SYNCHRONICITIES

While direct, two-way interaction with loved ones across the veil is a blessing, those in spirit can make their presence known in other undeniable and unforgettable ways. Because reality is relative, what is physical in our world is not so solid to those in spirit. When it serves the greater good, spirits can manipulate energy-information to give those here the experience of physical phenomena.

In my book, *Wolf's Message*, I describe how a young man in spirit named Wolf made a book on a bookstore shelf move to get my attention. The book appeared to shift to the left and then back to its original position. I even heard the sound of the paper brushing across the shelf. Was this real or an illusion? It was as real as any physical experience in my daily life, yet someone standing next to me might not have had the same experience.

I bought the book and discovered that it held an important message for me. This sign, an example of *physical mediumship*, accomplished the goal of getting my attention and encouraging me to take a specific, helpful action.

Many of my clients confirm physical signs that those in spirit report as their calling cards. These include:

- Flashing lights, often at meaningful times
- Objects falling from tables or shelves
- Electronic appliances and other devices coming on without physical intervention
- Telephones ringing with no one on the other end
- Text messages from unknown numbers with meaningful messages
- Candle flames flickering
- Objects such as coins or feathers appearing seemingly "out of nowhere"
- Flowers blooming at unusual times in unique configurations
- Important numbers showing up repeatedly on clocks, license plates, or elsewhere

One of the most common ways those in spirit get our attention is with unusual behavior by birds, animals, or insects like butterflies, dragonflies, and ladybugs. Loved ones who have passed may merge their consciousness with other creatures and with mutual agreement guide them to act in ways that attract attention.

My favorite example occurred after a young man in spirit showed me that he would send his mother an owl to let her know he was around. Later that week, she opened the front door of her house and was stunned when an owl flew past her. It continued up the stairs and landed in her son's bedroom. It stayed there for an hour until she had to gently shoo it back outside with a broom.

Spirit in all of its aspects is infinitely creative. Rarely does a day pass that I am not awed by a sign, synchronicity, or other communication event reported to me by my community or relayed to me in my own meditation or readings. This was not always true; I was a solid skeptic in the beginning. But I have learned to trust the information I receive. In the next chapter, you will read how you can put spirit to the test and how to address additional concerns that sometimes arise when we are first making the connection with Spirit.

# NO OTHER EXPLANATION

he thoughts and images that those in spirit project can be identical to the way your own thoughts sound and images appear in your mind. This causes those who are new to connecting with spirits to ask how to know the difference between imagination and what is real.

A wise being from the higher realms once told me, *You must stop differentiating between real and unreal. Do you not know now that angels and gods and archetypes are real? All is not as it seems.*

The more you investigate the nature of reality on the path of mediumship, you will come to know that the world is not as solid as it appears. What we see and experience may very well be a holographic projection of a deeper reality. Each of us creates our experience with consciousness. When we have shared experiences, we call this *reality*. When we create an experience that exists only in our own consciousness, we call this *imagination*.

The goal when connecting with a loved one across the veil is to discern information that relates to a shared reality. In the case of a private session or gallery reading, the medium wants to discern information known by the spirit that can be validated by their loved ones in the physical world. This is not always possible. Therefore, the important question is not, "Is this my imagination?" but "Is this helpful and healing?"

The easiest way to know that the communications from those in spirit are valid is when the information you are perceiving stands out from the normal thoughts and images that pass through your mind. Messages may arise abruptly, unexpectedly, and with more signal strength than your normal thoughts. When this happens, question if there is any reason for you to have had this thought or seen this image at this particular time.

When you see an image or hear a thought that does not seem to be your own, notice if you feel a presence and distinct personality. If so, engage in a conversation and observe how a response may arise.

In truth, when trying to connect across the veil, it is quite easy for the brain to spin a tale. The left hemisphere of the brain naturally pieces information together into stories. Through careful discrimination during moments of clear presence and undeniable evidence, you can learn to discern the difference between a fabrication and an actual presence.

# IS PROTECTION NECESSARY?

As a soul, you are a direct expression of Source. Darkness, including what we call evil spirits, is simply a lack of light. Darkness does not have its own power source. You don't fight something that has no true power. You bring in what is missing, meaning, you turn up your inner light and assert your dominion over any lower vibrations.

It is human nature to be fearful. The human body is hardwired for survival and responds automatically to threats with a response of fight or flight. When it comes to interacting with the non-physical realms, keep in mind that we do so from the level of the soul, beyond our human nature. The soul fears nothing, for it knows it cannot die.

Spiritually speaking, Franklin Roosevelt was correct when he said, "You have nothing to fear but fear itself." You attract into your field those experiences that you need to work through. If you are willing to look closely at fear when it arises, you will see that there is no substance to it. Fear is temporary. When observed, it flows through the energy field and dissipates. If resisted, fear will continue to arise until a particular challenge is observed and transmuted with awareness.

In mediumship, if connecting with the non-physical realms ever seems frightening, all that is necessary to dispel the darkness is to affirm the spiritual Law of Oneness. By stating, "I am the Light" and standing in that powerful state of awareness, you create a strong force field. You can then state, "Whatever presence may be here that is not aligned with the Light must completely leave my field now." Whenever any aspect of creation affirms its sovereignty in this way, all others must obey.

With this in mind, there is no harm in having a ritual in which you intentionally turn up your light before practicing mediumship. This is not done out of fear, but as an excellent practice to simply fortify your energy field on a regular basis.

# SETTING BOUNDARIES

It is important to respect and protect your energy field when working with spirits. Once you establish a connection with the higher realms, there is a tendency to want to keep the lines open. Alternatively, the spirits may be so pleased to find a new conduit through whom they can communicate that they drop in too often for the medium's comfort. For example, spirits may awaken someone in the middle of the night so often that it becomes disruptive to their sleep.

Just as with interpersonal relationships at the physical level, it is highly advisable to set up healthy boundaries with the spirit world. Using intention and will, you can lovingly state when an appropriate time is for those in spirit to make contact and what times are off limits. When you assert your personal power in this way, those across the veil are duty bound to abide by your wishes.

# THE IMPORTANCE OF EVIDENCE

I have already shared multiple examples of how those in spirit make their presence known by communicating details that a medium couldn't know. You will read about more beautiful after death communications in Part 2. These *no other explanation* moments and the information they convey are what makes evidential mediumship stand out from one in which only generic details and messages are delivered.

For someone who has no doubt that the afterlife is real and that the spirit survives bodily death, evidence might not be important. For those who may be skeptical of the existence of the greater reality but want desperately to know that their loved one has not simply vanished, it is evidence that heals hearts and changes lives for the better.

After my stepdaughter passed, I took my husband to see a medium. This was before I had any inkling that I would one day be communicating with spirits professionally and teaching others how to do so. If that medium had told me that she sensed a grandmother with gray hair around me who loved me very much, it's highly likely that someone else might have authored this book you're now reading.

Nothing but evidence would have convinced us that Susan was in the room with us. The things that medium told us after she reported the presence of a young woman in her twenties who died suddenly took us beyond doubt to knowing that Susan is still with us.

Some may claim there is no proof that those in spirit exist. While we may not yet have instruments to detect the presence of non-physical beings scientifically, evidential mediumship provides proof of the continuity of consciousness beyond bodily death.

In that first reading I attended with my husband, the medium provided proof far beyond a basic preponderance of the evidence. It was substantial and convincing, beyond a reasonable doubt. The only logical conclusion that could be drawn from that encounter and the information provided was that the medium was communicating directly with our Susan. She was right there with us in the room.

Having facilitated thousands of sessions filled with clear and convincing evidence, I can assure you that the greater reality is real. Mediumship offers the freedom and peace of mind that come from knowing that love never dies.

## GOING FOR "WOW"

The test of a good reading with a medium is that the client or "sitter" leaves the session saying, "That was my loved one!" If, for whatever reason, the connection is not good, a sitter may doubt that the medium was truly interacting with the person with whom they claim to be in contact. Clear evidence about the life of those in spirit can make the difference between doubt and knowing.

The challenge is that not all evidence is convincing enough to meet the test above. I learned this when mentoring a student medium, my friend, Brenda. I asked her to do a reading for a woman whose son had passed. Brenda seemed pleased with the session and told me that the woman could confirm almost everything Brenda sensed from her son.

I called the woman to receive feedback before listening to the recording. Based on Brenda's report, I was quite surprised when the woman did not share the same enthusiasm about the session. When pressed to explain her lack of confidence in the connection, the woman replied, "Almost everything

Brenda told me about my son was correct, but it also applied to three of my nephews who are in spirit."

This was an eye-opener for me, so I took careful notes while listening to the reading. Brenda had discerned a great deal of good information, but all of it was typical of a young American male. As a species, humans share character traits, emotions, and basic life experiences. Details can be particular to certain cultures, regions, and other categories that often result rightfully or wrongfully in stereotypes.

Brenda's reading had indeed earned an "A" for accuracy, but a big "G" for generic.

The things that make the difference between a client saying, "I'm not sure …" and "That was my loved one!" are those details that are unique to a certain person or uncommon enough that they stand out. I call these *differentiators*.

One standout detail can be all it takes to convince someone that their loved one is present. I recall having a reading with a medium who claimed to be connecting with my father. Everything she said either didn't fit him or was highly generic. I was about to dismiss the entire session when the medium said, "Now your dad is singing, 'I've been working on the railroad.'" With that one phrase, I knew my father was with us.

I would have preferred that the rest of the connection had been clearer, but she had passed the test. She could not have known that my father worked as a railroad engineer for forty-four years. If she had simply said, "railroad engineer," that would have been convincing, but the clever way in which he shared this gold nugget showed that the medium was not simply pulling data from the air.

Those in spirit want us to know they are present, and they will make every effort to provide evidence that distinguishes them from others. A good medium will push themselves to go for the "wows." They will ask those in spirit to provide as many gold nugget differentiators as possible and will not settle for less.

# BEYOND PROVING THE PRESENCE

"Wows" from evidence in a reading can change lives and even save lives. And yet, proving the continuity of consciousness is only part of the sacredness of mediumship. The other healing aspect of transdimensional communication is that it gives those who no longer have a physical voice the opportunity to say or show what they know their loved ones need to hear.

The biggest difference between a message and evidence is that we can't always validate personal messages. Here are a few examples of the kind of messages we can't prove until we cross the veil:

- "It's beautiful here."
- "I'm fine now."
- "I see you and visit often."
- "I didn't suffer when I passed."

You can imagine the comfort such communications can bring to bereaved loved ones. These types of messages have the potential to truly uplift us and provide the most hope and healing in a mediumship session. A medium knows they have discerned the spirit well when the loved one in physical form says, "That's exactly what I needed to hear!" or "They answered all of my questions."

The challenge is that messages, even more so than evidence, can sound very generic because they often relate to common emotions shared by all humans. The most frequently heard message that arises in a reading is, "I love you." From the soul's point of view, this is often the most important thing to communicate. Yet a grieving person might be tempted to think these are simply palliative words from a medium who wants them to feel better.

This is why it is important to balance messages with verifiable information about the spirit delivering them. The flow of evidence supports the conclusion that the message is, indeed, coming directly from the soul across the veil.

A message can include evidence when it relates to something that the recipient can verify. For example, a spirit who says, "I love you" may also show that they were never able to say these words aloud to their loved one and wish to do so now through the medium. Many spirits have told me, "These words may sound strange coming from me," and the client confirms that their loved one had never said these three important words aloud.

I am grateful that in communications with thousands of discarnate souls, I have never heard or sensed a meanspirited or hurtful message from across the veil. This is because spirits cannot help but feel the love that surrounds them once they're free of the body. They wish to share that Divine love and make up for any missed opportunities to do so. Mediumship allows them to do so.

When making a connection with spirits, a skillful medium will aim for just the right balance of evidence and meaningful messages. Those in spirit know which of their loved ones may be skeptical and they will naturally provide more verifiable information. Alternatively, a loved one across the veil will know when their loved one has no need for proof and will go straight to the heart with the messages they convey.

While it is not always possible to guarantee which type of communication will come through—evidence or messages—a medium can simply hold the intention that the greatest good be served through their interactions. Optimally, they will remain open to being the clearest possible instrument to best serve those on both sides of the veil.

In Part 3 of this book, I share helpful tools and techniques to fulfill this goal. Before you jump into the practices, however, I know you will thoroughly enjoy the stories in Part 2. In this next section, you will find examples of traditional one-on-one evidential readings such as those I write about in my two contributions. Most of the stories involve irrefutable after death communications with loved ones and even deceased pets. Each story was carefully chosen for their *no other explanation* moments of connection with loved ones who have passed.

Even though I regularly experience wondrous phenomena like those you will read here, I found myself saying "Wow!" and telling my husband, "You have to read this one!" I could feel a crowd of spirits around me as I read each sacred story. The pride and happiness each spirit feels at being included is tangible.

Despite the "wow factor," please be aware that these stories are not provided simply for your entertainment. They will delight you, for sure, and they may stir up powerful emotions. Most important from the big-picture perspective, they will gift you with the deep spiritual understanding that such interactions evoke.

You may find that you'll want to come back and savor the stories in Part 2 again and again. Please do so when you want inspiration and reassurance that the spirit world is real. By doing so, you will open to the possibility of similar types of experiences for yourself.

Are you ready to expand your belief system and open your heart and mind more widely to the spirit world? I know you are, so buckle your seatbelt and read on!

# PART TWO

*Sacred Communications with*
*Loved Ones from Across the Veil*

*Perhaps they are not stars in the sky, but rather openings where our loved ones shine down to let us know they are happy.*

— ESKIMO PROVERB

# BEYOND ANY DOUBT

*M*y client, Sally, showed up as I was carrying a load of food to the RV parked in front of our house. My assistant, Bev, had told Sally that I was in the middle of packing for a six-month trip. Through her tears, Sally apologized, but said she was desperate for a reading. Unable to say no to someone in such obvious despair, I had agreed to do the session on the spur of the moment.

I set the basket filled with non-perishables in the doorway of our motorcoach and led Sally into the house. We settled into two chairs facing each other in my study. Her back was to the window through which I could see my husband, Ty, loading tools and hiking gear into the storage bays of the bus.

After a few words about what to expect and how I work as a medium, I took Sally's hands and did a brief centering practice to bring us into resonance. When I shifted my awareness to the spirit world, I knew why Sally was so desperate for a reading. I sensed a young man in his twenties who I intuitively knew was her son, and he was eager to talk with his mother.

I couldn't see his features, but I could feel his masculine presence. As I sensed his unique personality and described it to Sally, I felt my own sense of sadness, knowing from our soul-to-soul connection how he had passed. When I told her that he was showing me that he passed by suicide, she burst into tears and wordlessly nodded her head.

I was instantly grateful that I had said yes to her request for a reading. I personally knew what it feels like to receive details from a medium about a loved one you are desperate to hear from. With that kind of life-changing evidence in mind, I asked the young man to provide me with information about himself and his passing that I couldn't have known.

In my mind's eye, I saw a hand going up and down in a wave-like motion. At that point in my mediumship journey, I didn't see the face or other physical characteristics of those in spirit who came to me, and I had learned to settle for what played out like a game of charades. I recognized the movement as a common symbol in my readings and interpreted it for Sally.

"Your son shows me a symbol that indicates he was bipolar. He tells me that he had medication to treat it, but his girlfriend didn't want him to take it."

"That's right!" she replied, wide-eyed.

"He's saying the name 'Matthew.'"

"That's him! That's his name!" Sally's hand flew to her mouth.

I sent a silent thank you to Spirit for this clear connection and continued. "He tells me he jumped from a bridge."

"Yes!" Sally said, clearly stunned. And then she asked, "Do you want me to tell you which one?"

"No," I replied, for even though I had no idea where Matthew lived at the time of his passing, he put in my mind the name of a well-known bridge thousands of miles from where we sat, which Sally immediately validated.

I felt as if she and I were swept into a vortex as the energy of this sacred gathering held us in close communion. The images and thoughts that Matthew put in my mind came with amplifying details that needed no words or visuals. I simply knew what he wanted to get across to his mother.

"Now he mentions a friend named Mark and he tells me they played in a band together."

Sally was no longer crying. She'd become caught up in the excitement of learning that her son was not "dead and gone."

"Yes!" she exclaimed. "Mark was his best friend. He feels so bad about Matthew's passing."

"Please tell Mark that Matthew loves the tattoo he recently got. It has something to do with music."

Sally jerked in surprise. She reached down and rolled up the sleeve of her striped cotton shirt, revealing a large tattoo on her left forearm with swirly script. "Mark and I got the same tattoo to honor Matthew. These are the lyrics to a song he wrote."

I sent another wave of gratitude to Spirit and prayed that I would never lose the awe of connecting so clearly with those no longer in a body.

Having validated Matthew's presence with the detailed evidence, I felt confident in accurately passing along the messages he wanted me to share with his mother.

"He says he's not burning in Hell—that there is great understanding across the veil for those who pass by suicide. He loves you so much and didn't mean to hurt you by leaving the way he did."

Like the ups and downs her son experienced, Sally shifted from smiling to sobbing once again. I gave her a moment to compose her emotions. As I paused, I realized that Matthew had not shared with me one of the specific pieces of evidence that I typically hear from those in spirit.

"Hey," I said silently to Matthew, "You didn't tell me what kind of work you used to do."

I deliberately communicated with him telepathically, knowing that if I asked Matthew about his occupation aloud, the answer would pass through Sally's mind. All mediums are psychic, and I didn't want to pick up the answer from her thought field. There was no need to use my psychic skills when Matthew was clearly in the room with us.

In answer to my question, Matthew once again reverted to charades, and I saw his hand sweep across my field of vision in an arc from left to right. He pointed outside the window behind his mother and replied, *"I used to do what your husband is doing right now."*

I glanced over Sally's shoulder, and I saw Ty kneeling down at the hitch we use to tow our car behind our RV. As I peered more closely, I could see that Ty was stripping wires for the brake light connection.

I smiled at Matthew's cleverness, knowing intuitively what he was trying to say.

I turned my gaze back to Sally and said, "Your son is showing me that he was an electrician."

"He was! That's what he did!" Sally affirmed excitedly.

I felt a thrill at this extra bit of evidence that I knew would help to alleviate Sally's grief. I then described for her the clever exchange that had led to this revelation.

"Do you see what this means?" I asked Sally to ensure that she understood the profundity of this magical moment. "He didn't just say, 'I was an electrician.' He showed me—by pointing out my husband's actions—that even though he is no longer in a body, he can see exactly what we are doing here."

Sally shook her head in wonder as I added, "Your son's body may have died, but he will be with you for all eternity. Love truly never dies."

Sally wiped away tears and sat back in her chair. She appeared tired, but visibly lighter than when she arrived. As she got up to leave, she thanked me profusely for taking the time when I had other things to do. I expressed my gratitude as well. Having no idea for most of my life that the spirit world is real, I knew that an evidential reading could instantly change the trajectory of one's grief.

I walked Sally to the door, but she stopped a few feet short and turned to face me. "You know," she said with gravity, "I may just have to start believing in God now."

Sally's words were my confirmation that the reading had passed the test of good mediumship. She was leaving the session with no doubt that we had just enjoyed a real-time, two-way conversation with her son and that he is still very much part of her life. Sally's world had been shattered by her son's passing, yet an actual verifiable visit with this young man across the veil had changed her life and filled her with hope.

*Suzanne Giesemann*

# LIKE THIS

On the day of my ninety-year-old mother's cataract surgery, she was afraid of so many things— floaters, being alone, the dark—that she asked me to stay with her overnight. I yearned to be home with my own family, but of course, I stayed. Even though our relationship was difficult, I was all she had in the world.

As I lay next to her in the bed, she and my father had shared for more than fifty years, I was tense, holding my body straight as a pencil, wide-eyed, barely breathing. After my vision adjusted to the blackness, tiny sparkles of light appeared and hovered above us, infinitesimal fireflies inhabiting her dark, dark room. My mother lightly snored next to me and I began to miss my father. Throughout my lifetime, he and I had been so connected, we could read each other's thoughts. When we were together, all was well. His love was unconditional, and his smile emitted pure love.

My father was my anchor, my hero, my confidante. When he was diagnosed with ALS, my life felt shattered.

About a year after his diagnosis, as his disease progressed in heartbreaking ways, I began settling into my new role as parent to my parent. I learned to feed him, help him get comfortable in bed, perform bathroom duties, and provide distraction and comic relief when I sensed his sorrow. We had time. The doctors said he'd live at least a few more years.

One afternoon, as I sat beside him on the bed regaling him with stories about my small children, he interrupted me:

"Shhhhh. Stop talking."

"Why?"

"Listen to me. I have a plan. I am determined to go."

*Wait. What?* "Go? Oh God, no. It's not your time, not yet. Where there's life there's hope, remember?" I started feeling dizzy and unmoored.

"I'm not going to get any better," he argued. "This is going to get worse and worse. You don't need to go through the pain of what lies ahead. I want to relieve you."

"I don't want to be relieved! I want *you*." I couldn't catch my breath, feeling like I was about to faint.

"My work here is done."

"No! What about me? You can't leave me." I nuzzled my head onto his chest and took in the scent of him, his flannel pajamas, the steady beating of his heart.

"You'll be fine. Your mother will be fine. Everyone will be fine. Sure, you'll cry for a little while, but then you'll cry less and less. Then you will realize that I am not really gone. I will be with you forever."

"But how will I live without you? How will I *feel you*?"

His soft strong hands cradled mine, and he said, "Like this. You will feel me just like this." He squeezed my hand, closed his eyes, and said no more for the rest of the evening. I tried to understand, but his words made no sense.

The next morning, I received a hysterical phone call from my mother. Dad had suffered a heart attack and was being taken by ambulance to the hospital.

"He cannot die, he cannot die, he cannot die," I robotically repeated as I sped to the hospital. When I finally arrived, I pushed my way into his room.

My mother wouldn't enter and remained standing in the hall. I found myself surrounded by people. They were talking and jabbing and poking him, roughly handling my father's beleaguered body. The scene looked violent rather than lifesaving. The erratic peaks and valleys of his heart monitor mirrored the chaos in the room.

He flatlined. The team met their marks like choreographed dancers and yelled "One, two, three, Clear!"— shocking and rocking and upheaving him in unnatural ways. The many surges and buzzes and violent movements made my bones and muscles lurch along with his. Between shocks, I held onto his legs for dear life.

The sight of my father's peaceful face stunned me. It seemed so utterly out of place amid this frenzy that, for the very first time, instead of weighty tomes of death, I heard silence, space, and love. *All will be well.*

I shouted, "Stop this! Please! Let him go!" and immediately realized my plea was contrary to every thought I'd had up until that moment.

Movement ceased. "He told me he wants to go," I explained, speaking slowly, each word carrying the weight of years past, present, and future. As the doctor and nurses turned toward the sound of my voice, my father's energy whooshed through my hands into my arms and moved throughout my body, shimmering, shivering, electrified, ecstatic. I loosened my grip. The blue line flattened. Transfixed by its calm, I felt the peace of a glassy blue lake in the mountains.

For months after his death, my senses were heightened in mystifying ways. The colors of nature were brilliant, almost neon. The cells in my own skin shimmered and moved like liquid gold. Pink roses pulled me into velvet swirling petals and as I inhaled, I became their fragrance. I knew in my bones my father was showing me a tiny slice of where he'd gone.

"This is what heaven smells like," my father had said to me years prior as he breathed in the perfume of a red rose. Now I understood.

I ran my hand through the air in front of me and felt it move through water, energy, or love. The world was alive with possibility.

After a few months, my sensory experiences waned, and I began to panic. Where had he gone? Years went by and I searched for them, and for him, grasping and worrying. Yet the harder I tried, the more elusive they became. I gave up hope of ever reconnecting with my father.

But on this night, lying in bed next to my mother, still holding myself as straight as a pencil, I finally fell asleep and had a dream that was not a dream at all. I was transported to the hospital room where my father had died, and I became the *him* on the hospital bed. He became the *me* holding his legs. I sensed the crashes and bashes on *his/my* chest as if they were muffled in slow motion. We were one person, underwater.

And once the storms around us quieted, together we rose up and up and up from that hospital room into the deep midnight-blue sky dotted with pinpricks of shimmering stars. And as we flowed into a trail of light, the air on my skin became soft velvet and my heart and body filled with such indescribable beauty that all of me dissolved and spread across the vast expanse of space, like gently rolling fog. We sensed and felt and became every atom within every molecule.

My father was guiding me, holding my hand. He had brought me into an ocean of love that was every thing and every place. The miracle of life, the heartbreak of death, the wind, the expansion and contraction of thought and breath—love is all of that, right here, right there.

My mother rustled, awakening me. I feigned sleep and through my half-closed eyes I watched her sit up and rock back and forth, muffling her crying like a frightened child. I'd never heard her cry, only yell. And I felt something new and soft, like love, for her. And that feeling filled the space between us, hugging us both.

I clasped my hands and knew without any doubt that yes, my father was holding my hand. He was right there, just as he'd always been.

I finally understood what he'd been trying to tell me all along: There is no separation, only love.

*Barbara Straus Lodge*

# THE PARTY CRASHERS

stare out the window on a gloomy February evening. A wave of "mom guilt" washes over me, as I have spent much of the day lost in my thoughts.

I call out to my son, Adam, offering to take him and his friend to the trampoline park, even though I'd rather curl up on the chair for the night. Surprisingly, the pair of voices call back, "No thanks!" followed by a chorus of overly dramatic wails. *Ah,* I think with amusement, *another Fortnight match lost.*

A gentle tug stirs within me. My thoughts return to my grandmother, Nanny, and her sister, my beloved great-aunt, Donna. We lovingly refer to the two of them as "the ladies." Inseparable, the ladies have lived either together or next door to each other their entire lives. Often mistaken for twins, they remain elegantly beautiful even in their late nineties. They now require round-the-clock care, but they are still together, sharing a room in a local care home. My heart aches with the thought that I will someday lose them.

These two women were like my second mothers, and I had the unique blessing of growing up in the same home as my Nanny and my grandfather, Poppy. My Aunt Donna lived next door along with my great-uncle and my great-grandmother. A big Italian family, our homes were always alive with laughter, cooking, and visitors.

Poppy passed a decade ago and I realize how lucky I am to have had the ladies in my life for so long. They have watched me become a wife and a mother to three children—Jack, Adam, and Caroline—and they have shared in the kids' daily lives as they grew. Visiting them in the care setting is painful, but I am grateful to be with them and bring them any joy I can in whatever time we have left.

Despite the cold and fast darkening February evening, I heed my instinct to visit them. I bundle up Caroline, my lively, free-spirited four-year-old daughter. She and her brothers always brighten the ladies' days, though they cannot manage much interaction anymore. I quickly stuff a Peppa Pig backpack full of crayons and activities to keep Caroline entertained.

Standing in the kitchen closet, I wistfully wish there were some way for the ladies to engage with her; how much they would have enjoyed this little girl if they were still well! A sudden thought comes and I reach for an old container of birthday party balloons tucked away on a shelf. I choose a bright yellow one, hoping they will feel up to batting it around with her. I grab some snacks, our coats, and off we go.

When we arrive, I am heartened to see Nanny and Aunt Donna still awake. Aunt Donna's eyes brighten as Caroline blazes into the room, throwing her coat off and emptying her backpack contents onto the bed. As I blow up the yellow balloon, Aunt Donna quips, "You sure got a lot of hot air!" I laugh at her sharp wit and spunky humor. She has been spending more time asleep than awake, so normal moments like this are precious. Caroline happily chatters away while she and the ladies swat the balloon back and forth. It is bittersweet to watch them, but I am so glad we came.

We stay longer than usual that evening, and although it's getting late, I impulsively add a trip to the cafe for some ice cream with Caroline and Aunt

Donna. Looking back, I realize that I didn't want to leave. Something told me that this night was important, and to remember every detail.

It would be the last time we were all together in this life. Aunt Donna took her last breaths little more than a day later. Nanny, never one to be separated from her dear sister, passed within a few months.

Eventually, the winter after Nanny's passing segues into the first days of spring, with Jack's birthday fast approaching. My heartstrings tug as I realize this will be the first birthday of many that the ladies will not be able to celebrate with us, and it already feels like a tough one.

On the eve of Jack's birthday party, I stand in my bedroom closet changing while Caroline watches a home movie she has randomly chosen from the plethora of DVDs in my cabinet. My eyes fall on the yellow balloon from that last evening together with the ladies. This tangible connection to them brings me comfort. I like knowing that each of our hands had touched it, Caroline's, mine, Nanny's, and Donna's. I close my eyes, place my hands on the balloon, and silently send the thought, *Please, if you're here, send me a yellow balloon.*

As I emerge from the closet, the home movie Caroline selected is still playing. I glance at the TV screen and gasp. There, in Nanny's kitchen, is Caroline, then aged nine months, along with Nanny, Donna, and Jack, all celebrating Jack's birthday. Tied to the kitchen chair is a single yellow balloon.

The next day, Jack's birthday cake is ready and the kitchen is decorated. Picking up my phone I text my mother, "I wonder if Nanny, Poppy, Aunt Donna, and everyone will show up at Jack's birthday party somehow?"

Quickly she responds, "Of course they will be with us in spirit!"

*Crash!* I am instantly jarred by a loud sound; something has fallen and smashed on the floor. I inhale a sharp breath and drop my phone. I am the only person downstairs. The boys are upstairs in their bedrooms playing video games. My heart pounding, a quick glance around the kitchen reveals nothing on the ground.

My mind races to Aunt Donna. In the days following her passing, the random, inexplicable noises around our home became a subject of great interest and speculation. "It's Donna!" I'd happily announce, with my husband looking bemused at my hopefulness. On this special birthday, could it really be that my loved ones were "crashing" the party?

I bound up the stairs, bursting into Adam's room. "Did you drop anything?" I frantically ask.

"No," he replies from his headset.

I knock on Jack's door. "Did something fall?" I ask him.

He glances up at me, and suddenly I'm aware of how bizarre I'm acting. "No Mom, nothing fell," he says.

It dawns on me that most of the upstairs is carpeted. Even if something fell, it would not make that crashing sound. I pointlessly continue to investigate upstairs, looking for the source of the loud crash. There is nothing.

Perplexed, my heart pounding in anticipation, I pad back downstairs. Room after room, I search. I'm about to give up when I realize I have forgotten the kitchen closet. I open the door and then I see it. There, on the hard tile floor, is a familiar container. It's the plastic bin with the balloons. I had not bothered with it since that February night, and now it had somehow fallen off the shelf. Impossibly, it lies on the floor upside-down, its lid popped off and askew underneath it.

*No one has been in here,* I think. *Logically, this makes no sense.* My body is now on full alert. There, peeking out from under the lid, lies a solitary yellow balloon, the only object thrown from the container upon impact.

My hand flies to my mouth and tears spring into my eyes. Whispers of love come alive all at once in my awareness, an instant download: *Happy birthday! Of course we showed up! Batting that yellow balloon around meant as much to us as it did to you.*

Something shifts then. A rush of exhilaration fills my body, and into my awareness pops, *So, is that a 'sign-y' enough sign for you?*

I laugh, allowing myself to feel their true personalities around me. In this moment, they are here, not as esoteric beings, but as my family, just as colorful and humorous as I'd always known them.

Bending down, I pick up the yellow balloon, and—still slightly shaking—blow it up. I bat it up into the air and, just as I would have in life, I give them a gentle ribbing. "Yes, that was 'sign-y' all right. Thanks for the yellow balloon… and for scaring the daylights out of me!"

*Kelly Beers Caprez*

# REMEMBER THIS

When my seven-year-old daughter Jocelyn was diagnosed with Lupus Erythematosus, it was a game-changer for my family. This disease knew no pattern and offered no promises, and we were all caught in its vortex. We had to figure out how to handle it day by day, episode by episode. Sometimes it brought stomach pain, or back aches, or nausea and discomfort. It often launched an arsenal of fears, both hers and mine. Lupus knocked me to my knees.

After three years of following doctors' recommendations and protocols, the ups and downs of this mysterious disease were exhausting us. We turned to Boston Children's Hospital, where Jocelyn endured extensive testing and medical consultation with a well-regarded, research-based team that worked with childhood SLE. The three-day visit left us feeling tired and defeated. Our hopes were dashed again. They could offer no cure for this chronic illness. The best we could do was to adjust her medications yet again and return to taking it "one day at a time." We had run out of places to look and no longer had any hope of a good outcome.

With a heavy heart, Jocelyn and I took our last day and walked to Quincy Market to shake off the medical world and just follow our fancy. We poked through free-standing shops, bought candies and treats, and heard some lovely minstrel music playing in the distance. The melodies called to us, and we headed in their direction. I lost myself listening to the sweet sounds, marinating with my nostalgia, while my daughter quietly stepped away from my side.

When she returned to me, she held a single pink rose in her hand, which she held out to me. She had spent her well-saved money at the flower vendor. Something about that tender gesture and poignant look between mother and child, spoke to my heart. I heard and felt a voice telling me, *Remember this moment.*

Two years later, Jocelyn passed. I was trying to come to terms with the loss of my daughter and the daunting task of trying to carry on. I was a single mom with a young son to raise. My faith was on the line.

A friend suggested that I work with a spiritual medium who might offer words of comfort. I didn't know what to expect, but I was a mother in pain, so I agreed to meet this man. I immediately sensed some kind of energy about him. As we prayed, hand over hand without touching, I felt a current of energy pulsing from his hand to mine.

When he entered a listening state, the first thing he told me was that a young girl was coming forward and she handed me a delicate flower. It was a single pink rosebud.

She had me at the rose. Jocelyn assured me that she was at peace. She could breathe easily. She was as close to me as my own breath, still sending me love through her beautiful, tender gesture.

*Linda Serway Bordwell*

# A SOFT PINK GLOW

*A* fierce blizzard blew outside while my sisters and I huddled next to our mom's bed, saying our final goodbyes. She died at the memory care facility in the same hospital where I was born and where my three brothers and three sisters were born. After the funeral, I caught a flight back to New York, arriving at LaGuardia about ten p.m.

While my cab driver surged through the late-night traffic, I was struck by the contrast of the cold, concrete skyline and my family farm's rolling hills. I enjoyed my single-woman life in New York, and I loved the pace and personality of the city. This night, though, I was numb with sadness. Mom had left us slowly, oh-so-slowly. She'd been diagnosed with vascular dementia fourteen years before she died. Her death was neither sudden nor unexpected. She'd had time to make her own funeral arrangements. She wrote her children a loving letter, reminding us to "be there for each other" and "seek harmony." And "don't pick out a casket that's too lavish." The letter was signed as usual: "I love you so, Mom."

As the cab drove me closer to my apartment building, I promised myself I'd bring out photographs and letters she'd sent me over the many years since

I left home. I wanted to feel her presence, to recall the many ways we'd stayed close.

I took the tiny elevator up to 3A, my one-bedroom haven on the Upper East Side. My mom's death was no surprise—so, why did my stomach gnaw with grief? I unpacked my suitcase, washed my face, brushed my teeth, and laid out an outfit for work the next day.

As I leaned against the side of the bed, I said out loud, "Mom, I miss you already. I believe you are in heaven. But how will we communicate?"

With no energy to look through old photographs, I crawled into bed, set my digital alarm clock for six o'clock, clicked off the bedside lamp, and sighed. "Well, maybe you can help me fix my chandelier. Good night, Mom."

The chandelier that hung in my bedroom was a treasure I'd found at a nearby used furniture store. The brushed brass branches of the elaborate fixture held flower-shaped, lavender glass bulb covers. Tiny teardrop crystal prisms hung from each of the seven branches. My neighbor, Liberty, who lived across the hall in 3D, had encouraged me to get it installed professionally. Liberty had grown up on Park Avenue, so I trusted her good taste in home decorating. Once the chandelier was hung, I asked her opinion. In her upper-crust, New York voice, she asserted: "Well, it's so *unattractive*, it's *attractive*. Keep it."

I did. When I returned from business trips, I'd click on my bedroom's main light switch and its soft pink hue greeted me every time—until one day it didn't. After flying in from a trade show, I clicked on the light switch and … no response, no light. Our building superintendent said it was beyond his scope and suggested an electrician. Liberty found a lamp repairman who made home visits, but his prognosis was not good: "Ma'am, it's dead. It needs all new wiring. That'll cost you $587.00." I'd decided to wait and get a second opinion on the repair.

At three a.m., I woke up to a soft pink glow filling the room.

"Wow, Mom, you did it! Thank you!" I exclaimed. I got out of bed and switched the chandelier off and then on again. And off again. It worked! My mother had fixed the chandelier! I went to sleep imagining her kissing me goodnight.

I had to share this minor miracle with Liberty. After work the next day, I called her to come over.

"Your mom just saved you over $500," she said with her dry wit.

"Yes!" I said, laughing and tearing up. "And now she's given me proof that she's with me, she hears me, and she loves me so."

*Mary Jane Klocke*

# MY MOTHER'S CHAIR

got the key from my cousin on a Friday morning. I'd held that same worn key between my fingerstips hundreds of times before, either sneaking in past curfew or letting myself in after school. The difference today was, I was forty-six and both my parents were gone, having died within eighteen hours of each other.

My three siblings and I grew up in this old farmhouse. It was built by relatives in 1830 and was the family homestead. It's where we gathered every Memorial Day and July 4th with aunts, uncles, and cousins, pulling Pepsis and Fanta orange sodas from ice-filled buckets. It's where we stood under the huge maple trees and gulped down charcoal-grilled hot dogs and barbequed chicken thighs, feeding the scraps to the barn cats when no one was looking. But that had been decades ago. The family gatherings dwindled once we grew up and moved away. We were busy making families and having picnics of our own.

My plan was simple. I was going to walk from room to room and soak in the atmosphere of the old house. I needed to breathe in the familiar smells of old wood, dusty books, and the musty scent that silently climbed the stairs from the dirt-floor cellar below. As I crossed the threshold, I heard the creak of the kitchen floor beneath me. That spot had given me away to my parents countless times in the early 1980s as I tried to slip into the house unnoticed.

Yes, I needed this time in this house, my old friend and a treasured part of the family. I wanted one last, grand sweep of the interior and exterior landscapes before everything changed. Losing my parents had compelled me to gather up memories like a squirrel does nuts when sensing the oncoming winter.

My folks had been gone for about nine months by then. My cousin's son had found my dad on the floor by his side of the bed, cold to the touch. A heart attack had claimed his life at eighty. My mother had died the next day in her hospital bed after deciding she'd had enough of this cancer stuff. I was with her when my sister Betsy called.

"Susan, the police just left my house," she said. "They came to tell us that Daddy's dead. You have to find a way to tell Mom."

Placing the phone back in my lap, I looked at my mother. Her face was slack, her brow unlined. She was peaceful now and resting on her back, the stark white hospital sheet pulled close to her collar bones, the slim tubes of oxygen doing for her what her lungs could no longer manage.

"Mom," I whispered, "that was Betsy. They found Daddy dead. Mom, Daddy's gone."

My mother locked eyes with me, the gray of her blue-gray irises sharpening as the words registered. Turning away, she looked out the window and murmured, "That son of a gun always said he would go first." She paused as if tasting the unexpected news before continuing.

"Hey, maybe we can have a double wedding. I mean, a double funeral. Oh, wait, I'm not dead yet! This is taking an awfully long time."

I was still struggling to wrap my head around the news and muttered something ridiculous about trying to relax when she commented, "This morphine is really good stuff."

Hearing that and knowing she was no longer in physical pain made me feel better. "I'm glad, Mom."

There was no reason not to relax and enjoy the feeling. After finding a hospital pen and a scrap of paper, I sat back down at her bedside, and we set about planning her and dad's double funeral.

Mom wanted "Sunrise, Sunset" from *Fiddler on the Roof* to be played at the wake and for Dad, she also chose Frank Sinatra's "When I was Seventeen."

"He's always been a sucker for that one," she said.

I made a few more notes and she confirmed where her written funeral arrangements were. Without saying so, I knew we were done. I couldn't ignore that, in those brief, intense moments, she had grown noticeably wearier.

"Are you the only one?" she asked.

I knew she was asking, "Is anyone else planning to come by and watch while I die?"

I assured her that I was it, and she brightened and said, "Oh good! Now give me a hug." Leaning in, I felt the softness of her round cheek pressing against mine and she whispered, "Oh, you smell so good. I'll see you later."

Gathering up my things, I told her again that I loved her, but it wasn't until the elevator doors closed that it hit me. She hadn't meant, I'll see you tomorrow, next week, or at Christmas dinner. This time, "I'll see you later" had meant, "I'll see you on the other side."

Walking through the old house now felt like slipping through a portal. Suddenly, I was ten again. I plopped down on the rust-colored sofa where'd I'd sat countless times poring over my siblings' yearbooks, trying to imagine how cool high school would be. Betsy and I had spent so much time in that living room practicing our instruments, doing homework, bickering, and challenging each other in the Thanksgiving tradition of who could hold a black olive in their mouths the longest before spitting it out.

The house was so quiet now. I tried to ward off the feeling of disappointment. I'm not sure what I'd expected, but this wasn't it. All at once, I felt depressed and like a little orphan girl.

I stared through the big bay windows that stretched from floor to ceiling and replayed old tapes in my mind. Riding my cousin's hand-me-down bike, speed skating on the ice-covered driveway, hiding in the trees and playing in the dwindling summer light.

Picking myself up, I moved into my parents' downstairs bedroom. My despair was replaced with immense gratitude for having had such a sweet and simple childhood.

Like most of us, my parents were creatures of habit. They were married for sixty-two years, and each had a favorite chair they parked themselves in. I wandered over to my mother's chair and perched on the edge of the cushioned seat. My breath caught in my chest as my eyes took in ten or twenty strands of her snowy white hair still clinging to the upholstered headrest.

Sinking onto the floor, I felt the stinging rush of unexpected tears. It hadn't occurred to me that I'd encounter something so tangible, so undeniably *her*. Just like that, the calm Swedish exterior we were raised to project gave way like a little kid's sandcastle to the rising tide.

*Dear Lord, that chair is filthy!*

It was my mother's voice. I would have recognized it anywhere! And it would be just like her to point out the practical, in the midst of the emotional.

Standing up, I wiped my face with my sleeve and had to laugh. "Okay, Mom, I hear you," I said aloud. "I was just having a little moment. Can't I have a little moment?"

Directly behind me was a set of wooden shelves that my father had built years before. One of the shelves had a long row of books that I hadn't noticed before. They were all old and nearly identical except for height and breadth. Without any conscious thought, I reached out and grabbed a nondescript, tall, slim volume. I randomly opened it and traced my finger down about halfway on the page.

"The red, red rose was in her hand, The tear was in her eye, I said: I come from Dixieland, Susan-na don't you cry."

I stood there, shaken. *Junior Laurel Songs*—the book was filled with notes in Mom's little-girl handwriting from the late 1930s.

Out of that long row of plain brown books, she'd not only led me to the right one, but to the exact song, out of 152 songs, and the one verse she knew would leave no doubt in my mind. That song was "Oh, Susanna" on page 13. There was no better way she could have impressed upon me, "Susan, I am fine. There is no need to cry."

So, I pulled up my britches, as Mom would say. I dried away more tears and laughingly conceded, "Okay, Mom, I hear you loud and clear." With one last, sweeping look around my beloved childhood home, I felt a new lightness in my heart.

And why not? We were going to be seeing each other later, after all.

*Susan Ferling Poole*

# MAHALO HOUR

n 2016, my husband Greg and I went on a dream-come-true kind of trip to Australia, first traveling from Nepal and Indonesia to Cambodia and Singapore. Greg immediately fell in love with Australia.

"How can we manage to stay here?" he wondered out loud.

We first spent time in Sydney, enchanted by its sparkling harbor, the cockatoos, and the eucalyptus trees. Then we traveled up to the Sunshine Coast where we climbed a small, sacred mountain, Mount Coolum. One morning, about two weeks after we arrived, Greg announced he was going for a walk and promised he would return in an hour.

He never came back.

I called the police and filed a missing person's report. The search and rescue teams were called. For three days, the search carried on. Neither the Queensland Police Search and Rescue teams nor the infrared helicopters could find any trace.

During the heavy, stressful days while he was missing, I had the prescient feeling that he was out of his body, but I couldn't be sure. I didn't receive any clear communications or clues. I realized that, if the news was bad, part of me didn't want to know.

On the morning of the fourth day—just before they would have called off the search—an off-duty police sergeant decided he would clamber around the cliffs at the base of Mount Coolum. In an area where the search parties hadn't gone, he discovered Greg's body at the bottom of a cliff. He had fallen and died instantly of massive head and chest trauma.

"We searched his bag and found his wallet, passport, and a bus ticket leaving for Mount Coolum at 8:27 that morning. We also found a pack of cigarettes with four cigarettes missing," the police reported.

After I got his ashes back, I began to receive some peculiar messages from Greg. He always loved to have his beer right at five p.m.— "Mahalo hour," he called it. He'd drink a beer or two, smoke a couple of cigarettes, and relax while he watched the sunset.

On October 15th, I took the train from Brisbane back up to the Sunshine Coast, bringing Greg's ashes back from the crematorium. I planned to spread some of them near Mount Coolum. Because of the weekend schedule change, however, I had missed the earlier train and had to travel in the heat of the afternoon. I was exhausted and dozed off.

A strange sound woke me up—something lurching around on the floor. I opened my eyes and noticed a bottle rolling back and forth, directly in front of my seat. I picked it up. It was a full bottle of beer! And, because of missing the earlier train, it was exactly five p.m. when the beer appeared.

Mysteriously, the train car was empty. "It's Mahalo hour on the train!" I excitedly said to Greg. In a bit of shock, I stashed the bottle in my backpack.

The next day, after spreading some of his ashes in the thick bush around the base of Mount Coolum, I was walking back on the sidewalk near the golf course when I saw a pack of cigarettes lying on the ground. It looked out of place, with nothing else around. I walked closer. I thought the pack was empty, but—to my surprise—when I picked it up, there were exactly four cigarettes in it. That's the number Greg had smoked on his last day.

*It's so odd*, I thought excitedly. *Why would I find a package with four cigarettes?* I knew it must be a sign from Greg. *Very funny, Greg. Cheers. Keep the messages coming.* And he has.

That night, I went back to the motel, and at Mahalo Hour, I took a photo of the pack of cigarettes and the unopened bottle, raised a toast to Greg, and drank the beer.

*Marya Corneli*

# MARIA

*H*er voice was urgent as she asked me to come. When I got to her house, she made me sit down. With firm conviction in her voice, she said, "I had a dream. I learned that I will die very soon!"

I couldn't help but laugh at her news. Maria was my healthy, beautiful grandmother. In her mid-eighties now, she was still slim, tall, and elegant. Her mind was sharp, and she remained extremely fair, thoughtful, and caring. I could listen to her stories for hours.

My grandmother had lived an interesting life. As a volunteer partisan during WWII, she had been captured by the Nazis and had survived a concentration camp, never returning to her home in what is now known as Belarus. Her first husband, Tony, had been the love of her life. He was a Czech who had also been captured and barely survived a concentration camp. They met after the war as immigrants in Australia.

Tony died suddenly on her forty-sixth birthday. She never celebrated her birthday again.

Now she was describing her dream and saying she might die in three days, or three weeks, or in three somethings.

I asked, "But why?"

"In my dream, I saw Tony dancing with me in my living room, holding me so tightly and lovingly. When he gave me a big smile, I looked at his young, handsome face and suddenly realized that he was missing three teeth in the front!"

In the superstitions of her culture, she said, missing teeth meant "death," and the number three was an indication of the time she had left.

I was completely skeptical, since Maria was a vibrant, joyful woman. She constantly worked in her yard, cooked three elaborate meals every day, and would briskly walk around the neighborhood. When we walked together, I could barely keep up! There was no reason for her to even consider thoughts of death.

"Maybe your dream could be interpreted in a different way," I argued.

"I know what I saw!" she said as she placed in front of me a notepad with neatly handwritten and detailed directives, all the instructions I would need to follow upon her passing.

A few days later, her skin started turning yellow. Doctors said it was a bile duct tumor. She refused the suggested surgery and treatment medications, saying, "I want to die in my own bed." I arranged hospice care and hired a sitter for her, to honor her wishes.

Weeks passed, and she started to decline. She was not able to eat but remained stoic and dignified. She never complained.

I lived and worked an hour away from her home, but I oversaw her care. One Thursday, I asked the hospice nurse to be at Maria's house at eleven a.m., so we could discuss her care plan and what medications she might need if she started experiencing pain. Maria had repeatedly told me that she had no pain—a miracle, given her condition—but I wanted to be prepared to make her more comfortable if that time came.

Maria didn't know I had made this appointment with the nurse.

Yet on the Wednesday before I arrived, Maria said to her helper: "I will die tomorrow morning at eleven!" Nobody took that seriously.

On that Thursday morning, I was delayed at work and left twenty minutes later than I had planned. I was heading for her house, driving on the highway, when I received a panicked phone call from Maria's caregiver.

"I think Maria is dying! Her breathing is very rapid, and she's not responsive."

It was eleven a.m.

"Put the phone next to her ear," I said. I started talking to Maria while speeding to her house, which was still several minutes away. I told her that I was coming and would see her soon, and that I loved her. Although she was not responding, I felt she was listening.

Suddenly, the caregiver took the phone and exclaimed, "She is breathing more normally now. I think she stopped dying."

When I rushed inside the house, I found Maria peacefully lying in her bed. The moment I took her hand into mine, her breathing again became erratic. Her eyes opened and scanned the room as if she was seeing something amazing. She didn't pay attention to any of us, but looked as if she was engaged in something unique.

The nurse, who was also late, arrived a few minutes after me. She looked at Maria, nodded, and said, "She is transitioning."

We all sat by Maria's side, and I held one of her hands. I told her how much I loved her.

"You're going to heaven, and you'll meet and be surrounded by all your loved ones there, including Tony." I don't know why I was saying all of that. It felt as if something was speaking through me.

When she took her last breath, a potent feeling of endless, powerful love began rushing through my chest. I felt my heart expanding, ready to burst. It was almost impossible to breathe. I felt as if I was saturated and filled with beautiful, unconditional, radiant love and gratitude. I experienced exuberant, elevating joy. These feelings were so powerful, and I felt so intoxicated with this love and joy, that I almost didn't notice the other people crying in the room. I felt I should be ashamed of these astonishing feelings while everyone else was struck with grief, but I wasn't.

Even when I called my mom and told her about Grandma's passing and shared my unusual feelings, she couldn't understand what I was talking about.

A few hours later, I was pulling out of Maria's driveway to begin the long drive home. The moment I sat in the car and turned my car key, the radio spontaneously started playing a song: "Ave Maria." I assumed that my car stereo had automatically connected to my iPhone play list, but I could not believe it was the first song after Maria's departure!

Driving and listening to the song in shock, I felt certain that Maria was communicating with me. When the song came to an end, to my compete astonishment, a second "Ave Maria" by a different artist started playing. The odds of this happening randomly seemed astronomical! But then when the second "Ave Maria" ended, a *third* one played—and after that, a fourth one! I had no idea that there were that many versions of the song played by different artists. But the fact that I had all four in my phone, and that they all played in a row …

I realized then that it had been exactly three months since her prophetic dream.

The next morning, I had to be at a conference that I'd signed up for months earlier. I was already starting to feel all the normal human emotions of my grandmother's passing: grief, sadness, and a huge sense of loss. But I decided I would attend the start of the conference, out of respect for the organizers. I planned to tell them that I would not be attending the rest of the event.

The morning reception was held in a big hall. The participants were starting to gradually gather, but I stood by the wall alone, unable to socialize. In the periphery of my vision, I saw a young woman who kept turning and looking at me. She was slim and well-dressed with long, blond hair and deep brown eyes. Eventually, she crossed the room and stood right in front of me.

Her name tag said "Pamela." I'd never met her before. She introduced herself and bluntly asked: "Did you lose someone in your life recently?"

I was stunned. I said, "Yes, as a matter of fact I did, just yesterday."

"Her name started with an 'M', something like Maria?"

"Yes, Maria. She was my grandmother."

"She has a message for you".

Looking at this woman in disbelief, I replied hesitantly, "Okaaay... a message?"

"Yes, she wants you to know that she has arrived and she is surrounded by her loved ones. She also wanted you to know that she was waiting for you yesterday."

I knew what she meant: Maria had delayed her death until I came to her bedside.

"But why?" I asked.

Pamela replied: "Maria said that she just wanted you to know that there is no death."

*Irina Melnik, MD*

# LOVE NEVER DIES

I stumbled blindly out of the building, wracked with aching sobs, feeling the unbearable grief of loss. The sobs and gasps trickled into quiet ... and then everything changed.

Moments before, I had gazed upon the gray, still form of my partner's sweet sister and dear friend, someone I had hoped to know forever. Michelle had been brilliant, spiritual, and creative. She was one of those people who seemed larger than life. I couldn't imagine that she could ever disappear, to ever not be here to take care of everyone and everything. I expected her to grow in magnificence, inspiring us with her greatness.

But she was gone, in the blink of an eye, the victim of a motor vehicle accident. Her entire family had been in the car she was driving, but her three young children and husband survived.

It was clear that the person I loved was no longer in the small, colorless shell of her body. When I tried to feel her there, I was met with a hollow silence. But as I stepped outside, I felt Michelle briefly opening the doorway between the worlds, allowing me a glimpse of where she was.

As I slowly started to breathe again, I looked around. The colors seemed so vibrant now, the lilies lining the steps so brilliant. I sat down in front of the funeral home's pink-marbled walls and noticed the way the sunlight filled the afternoon, making a blinding reflection off the stones.

Seagulls swept the sky and cried out. A soft, heavy humidity full of briny air filled my nose and lungs. In the heavy dampness, my skin felt open and warm. Incredulously looking around at the world that continued to exist, despite my unbearable tragedy, I had never felt so present in my life.

Then Michelle lifted the veil between the worlds and showed me she was more alive than ever. It was a glimpse that shook all my perceptions and erased my previous beliefs about life and reality.

The light changed, and as far as I could see, a golden light surrounded everything and infused all people, objects, nature, and the air with large golden spheres of light. The light was pure love, and love was the light.

My deep, unbearable grief fell away from me as if disappearing down a dark shaft into the earth. My body felt free as the world opened around me, filling me with awe.

I felt Michelle's presence, heard her laugh, and say, *You must tell them I am alive.*

And in that moment, she was more real than anything I'd yet experienced in life.

Grief's gifts can be transformative and catastrophic. Michelle's death was a wake-up call. I saw that my life was something I'd barely dipped my toes into, allowing fear to hold me back. Now I felt the possibilities: What if I jump in, embrace my existence, and live without fear, knowing the light permeates all existence and that love, like life, never dies.

*Celia Chantal*

# A SIGN FROM DAD

I arrive just before midnight. The hospice room is dimly lit. Lying beneath white bed sheets, hooked up to an oxygen machine, is a pale, emaciated version of my dad. When I approach the bedside and gently touch his hand, his eyes slowly open. A smile of recognition flickers across his face. In that moment, I feel total relief. After a four-hour flight and two-hour drive, I made it in time.

The nurse who ushered me into the room softly announces, "Mr. Earl, your youngest is here." She leaves.

"Hi, Dad. It's Bonnie."

Another feeble smile.

"I hear you've been having quite a time."

He nods, followed by a long silence. I gather my composure, unsure what to say next. Finally, I gain the courage to ask the unspeakable.

"Are you ready to go, Dad?"

"Yes," he responds in a whispery voice.

"Are you worried about Mom?"

"Yes."

"You know that Wilma, Don, and I will take care of her."

With labored breath punctuating each word, he answers, "That's ... the most important ... thing."

My mom and dad had celebrated their sixtieth wedding anniversary a month earlier. Part of me wondered if, having reached that milestone, Dad had decided he could leave now, without letting Mom down.

"You know, Dad, I am feeling done, too. Done with my job." Dad's steady gaze tells me that he needs to hear more. "I've had a long and fulfilling career, but since my husband's death, I've been restless. Many things I once thought significant no longer hold the same importance. I feel like it's time to close this chapter. I'm yearning to share the precious life lessons I've been given."

My dad closed and opened his piercing blue eyes, squeezing my hand for emphasis and answered, "Just ... do it."

In that late night, heart-to-heart exchange—with the rhythm of an oxygen machine in the background, reminding us of the fragility of life—an indelible bond was forged. Two souls gave each other permission to break free: one from an incurable condition, the other to pursue a soul's calling in a new direction.

The white, sterile hospice room became my home for the next two days. The black leather loveseat was my bed. Other family members came and went, but I remained Dad's gatekeeper.

At one point, as the hours dragged on, Dad looked at the large clock mounted on the wall at the foot of his bed. With the frail pointer finger of his right hand, he made several clockwise motions to depict the agonizing moments passing. He was ready to go.

Finally, around seven a.m. on October 2, 2004, my father's struggle ended. There was no fanfare. Just the two of us in a sterile white room, a thin, raspy, inhalation... and no exhalation. I did not see his soul depart, but I viscerally felt it. One moment, Dad was there. The next, he was not.

As I looked at my dad's now-lifeless body, a strange mixture of sadness and relief washed over me. Mostly relief. After a decade of living with one lung, following his cancer surgery, his struggle to breathe was now over.

I walked to the window, opened the blinds, and turned my back on death. A gentle rain was falling. Below the hospital window, between the building entrance walkway and parking lot, stood a deer. As she gracefully grazed on some grass hidden beneath a covering of fallen maple leaves, she seemed completely unconcerned about cars or people passing by. Her presence seemed natural. I saw it as a welcome sign of reassurance that Dad was at peace.

I continued to have conversations with my dad. Sometimes I asked for advice. His responses were always clear and simple with a gentler, more encouraging tone than I remembered growing up. Sometimes I would share family news. After each conversation, I'd feel comforted, with a sense that he was still watching over me.

But, on August 27, 2021, on what would have been dad's ninety-fifth birthday, I longed for a concrete sign.

I decided to take a short road trip, a spontaneous adventure. As I drove solo to a nearby town, I experienced an outpouring of emotions. On this day, I felt compelled to share aloud my deep gratitude to my father for who he was and what he had meant to me, along with a fervent prayer.

"Thanks for being the best dad I could ever hope for. Thanks for always being there for me, for your constant love and support." With tears in my eyes, I pleaded, "Dad, I know you hear me, but I would really like a sign. Would you please give me a sign that you have heard me?"

With my heart full of gratitude and longing, and my dad's name on my lips, I felt drawn to my favorite antique store, a 15,000-square-foot treasure trove of hidden gems. For the next forty minutes, I wandered through aisles lined with vintage curiosities, old photographs, and antique furniture. The store was a labyrinth of other people's memories, each item holding a piece of someone's history. I was overwhelmed by the sense of nostalgia and the silent stories that lingered in the air.

I continued to explore, losing myself in artifacts of the past, until something extraordinary caught my eye. I turned a corner, looked up, and stopped dead in my tracks. There, in bold black letters, I saw a sign that seemed to shimmer with light. It was a large metal sign suspended from the ceiling by wire, bearing two names: Bill and Earl. Tears welled up in my eyes. My mouth hung open in amazement as I stared at the sign. The odds of finding a sign with my dad's first and last names—among the gazillion items in this vast antique store—seemed too incredible to comprehend. I looked at the back side of the sign. It also bore Dad's first and last name: Bill Earl.

In that moment, I knew my pleas had been heard from beyond the veil and that Dad was still watching over me with love and care. I felt a profound sense of comfort and elation, as if a warm embrace from the other side had enveloped me. I had asked for an irrefutable sign ... and forty minutes later, a literal, tangible sign was delivered.

I purchased the Bill Earl sign and carried it home as a physical reminder of our beautiful connection that transcends time and space. That sign continues to be a cherished symbol of the eternal bond between father and daughter, a testament to the belief that loved ones never truly leave us.

*Bonnie Earl*

# TELL HER I LOVE HER

The ring of our landline at 6:30 in the morning sounded ominous. The only person who used that number was my mother, and it was far too early for her to be calling. Minutes later, I melted into a puddle on the bathroom floor, praying for God to evaporate me straight to heaven to be with my dad.

The finality of death streamed down my cheeks in miserable tears. Never again would I hear his gloriously joyful laugh or feel one of his warm, Lagerfeld-scented hugs. No more of his sage medical advice or his whistling as he came down the stairs. No more Thanksgivings with Mom and Dad's perfectly choreographed routines, as comforting as hot cocoa on a crisp, autumn eve.

My husband ushered our kids down the hall so they wouldn't hear my desperate, pleading sobs. But I knew they sensed the pain anyway. Feeling their innocent, tender hearts crumble with the news of their Papa made me cry harder.

I hurried to the kitchen, where my phone was charging on the countertop of the butler pantry, and with trembling hands felt I had to send one last text message to my dad. I'd hoped that from wherever he was, he could see me.

Since the kids had school, and I knew there would be lots of family coming and going at Mom and Dad's house, we made plans to visit during the upcoming spring break. Time passed in a haze of grief, and then I was sitting on the edge of Mom and Dad's bed hearing her recount the events of the night he'd passed in his sleep.

Mom gestured to the items of his on the nightstand. "I haven't moved any of his things yet," she said. The nightstand was an untouched shrine in his honor. A pair of drugstore reading glasses, a few bottles of prescription medications from the surgery he'd had only days before he died, and a box of tissues he'd left behind… and his new iPhone.

"Leah, take whatever you want," Mom said. "Take his phone."

It didn't feel right to disturb any of Dad's things; they seemed to belong in Mom's little makeshift museum. But after more urging on her part, I decided to choose a few things to remind me of my beloved father: the reading glasses that used to stick out of his well-pressed shirt pocket, a handkerchief—which mom spritzed with his signature cologne—and Dad's cell phone.

Weeks went by, and the only person who really did anything with Dad's phone was my son, Rhy. He'd play games on it, or just sit on the couch and scroll through the photos and messages.

On Memorial Day of that same year, I was standing on a stepladder wiping off the top of the refrigerator and chatting with Rhy, who was leaning against the pantry wall with my dad's phone in hand.

"Oh, Mom," he said, softly. "I can see the message you sent to Papa the day that he died."

"It was right after Nana called with the news," I said. "It was all I could think to do. I was so desperate to reach him somehow." I felt slightly embarrassed, and grateful that no one else in my family had seen my text.

Rhy read the message back to me, as though I hadn't heard it before. "I love you, Daddy. Xoxo. And Mom… there's a reply."

I stopped what I was doing and turned to face my fourteen-year-old son, a tingling sensation running up and down my arms and a familiar weakness returning to my legs.

"What do you mean, a reply?"

It says, "Tell her I love her."

My heart leaped into my throat as I climbed carefully down from the stepladder, my vision blurred with tears. My dad's text from beyond is the greatest comfort to my still-aching heart.

*Leah Polaschek*

# FRAGRANT REMINDERS OF LOVE

*L*oose gravel crunched under the tires as I drove down the rolling country road toward my childhood home. A visit with my parents had always filled me with joyous anticipation, but today, I was sad. I knew I would find only one person awaiting me, my mom. For three days, I had driven to assist mom with the funeral arrangements for my beloved father. Today, I would gather with my family at the homestead before driving to the country church for a final good-bye to our patriarch.

I remembered how Daddy looked when he came through the front door after a hard day's work in the tobacco fields: the prickle of sunburn on his neck, sweat dampening his face and hair, and the red dust of the fields coating his clothes and shoes.

As I passed by the front of the house, I caught a glimpse of Mom standing in the doorway, eagerly awaiting my arrival. I turned into the gravel drive and steered to the right, the side Daddy had used when he was healthy and able to drive, although it was now covered under a thick thatch of weeds. I didn't stop until the hood of my car was shaded from the summer sun by the low hanging shed roof of the old garage.

After I turned off the engine, I sat in the car, savoring the moment: windows down, deeply inhaling a mixture of clean air, oil, gasoline, and the dry smell of dust as it wafted down from the pole-beam rafters. Memories of all the wonderful times I had spent with my father in the garage flooded back.

I had been Daddy's little girl, his shadow. While he worked, invariably he would turn to find me standing in the open doorway, chewing on a stalk of sweet grass and watching his every move. He would greet me with a smile and wave me in, welcoming my company and my never-ending questions. Sometimes, we simply shared the silence of the countryside that was occasionally interrupted by the distant clank of a tractor or the mooing of cows grazing nearby.

I imagined him sitting on the locust stump, wearing his Red Camel overalls as he casually puffed on his cherished briarwood pipe. Watching the unhurried, methodical act of him drawing smoke through the pipe was meditative and calming.

How fascinating it was watching him perform the ritual of packing and lighting the pipe! First, he would carefully remove the pipe from the front breast pocket of his overalls, pull his trusty pocketknife from his side-pocket, and open the blade. He'd wind the knife's blade tip around the inside of the pipe to remove the ash and hardened tobacco residue. Next, he would tap the pipe against his hand several times, dropping the spent tobacco onto the ground. Then he'd reach back into the front breast pocket and retrieve his favorite blend of tobacco: Middleton's Cherry, moist and sweet, in the white foil pouch with the red-scripted, oval-shaped label. He would pack the bowl to the rim and firmly press the tobacco down with his thumb. Finally, it was time to light the contents with a wooden stick match he struck against a piece of wood. The sharp, phosphorus smell of the match would linger in the air until it was displaced by the tobacco's sweet cherry aroma.

The cry of a hawk flying overhead, on the hunt for a mouse or lizard skittering through the grass in the adjacent field, roused me from my reverie. I climbed out of the car, closed the door behind me, and stepped onto the lawn. Before I could go any further, a shiver curled through the hairs on the back of my neck and cascaded down my backbone, immediately followed by the flicker of a shadow at the corner of my vision.

I froze, unable to move, as I caught the scent of *cherry* in the air. Could it be *tobacco smoke*? The fragrance was undeniable, growing stronger every second until I was surrounded by the sweet, ripe smell. Cherry pipe tobacco! I felt Daddy's presence all around me like a warm hug, filling my soul with love and light.

I slowly turned and walked back to the garage entrance, hoping beyond hope to find Daddy sitting on the old locust stump, puffing on his pipe. I peered in and saw shadows clustering at the back of the enclosure, a product of the sun's western slant toward the horizon. As my vision adjusted to the shadow-streaked darkness, I could see that the old stump was empty. My eyes began to glisten with tears—but then a smile emerged. I had been given a gift! Daddy had reached out to tell me, "I am not gone, I'm still with you!"

I ran to the house and shared the wonderful news with Mom. Her face lit up. We both knew without a doubt that we had received a message from Daddy! We embraced and were happily weeping just as the rest of the family began to arrive.

Now, twelve years had passed since that summer day when Daddy returned to his eternal self. Spring had arrived and, once again, I was back at my childhood home. As I surveyed the surrounding countryside, I savored the fresh touch of the breeze on my face, the new shoots of green grass beneath my bare feet and the sun's warmth on my skin. This was the first spring without Mom, and although I missed her terribly, I found comfort knowing she and Daddy were finally reunited.

My parents had been wed in 1935 during the Great Depression, a time when most of my family had lost their sources of income, leaving them challenged and changed. But my parents' wedding made the future look bright, instilling a sense of hope that had been lacking for a long time.

The ceremony itself was a simple affair, held at the local country church. Daddy wore his only suit, a navy blue seersucker, and mom wore her best Sunday dress. My mother's head was adorned with a handmade bridal veil fashioned from a piece of lace that her mother had saved for years.

The reception was in the front parlor of my maternal grandparents' home. My aunt made the wedding cake—her famous homemade sponge cake with confectioner's icing—which was served with Grandma's iced tea, sweetened with honey from Grandpa's beehives.

My grandparents gifted them a one-night stay at a popular mineral springs resort in the Sauratown Mountains of North Carolina. The happy couple headed for their honeymoon in Grandpa's 1925 Model T Ford.

Mom had recounted the details of that evening many times during my childhood, her face animated and eyes aglow. It had been the first time in her life she had stayed in a hotel, and she said it was the most beautiful and picturesque place on earth. The food, which was served buffet style, was the best she had ever eaten. She and Daddy ended their meal with cups of coffee and slices of pecan pie, and that's when my daddy pulled a small box from the inside pocket of his suit jacket. The box was wrapped in plain brown paper and tied with a red ribbon. He placed the box in the middle of the table and gently took Mom's hand, vowing to love her always.

Mom excitedly untied the ribbon and pulled away the brown paper to expose a delicate, cobalt blue cardboard box inscribed with "Evening In Paris." Inside was a beautiful cobalt blue bottle of Evening In Paris perfume nestled in satin. She had never seen anything so beautiful nor smelled such a fragrant and delicate perfume, a bright mix of violets, roses, and carnations with a hint of vanilla. From that day forward, Evening In Paris was my mom's favorite perfume.

The undeniable reality of the chore that lay before me, packing and moving the content of Mom's life, snapped me back to reality. This was not going to be easy, but at least I had a beautiful spring day in which to achieve the task. I deliberated on where to begin, what to pack first and what to leave for another day. The task suddenly felt overwhelming.

Instead of diving in, I couldn't help but enjoy the surroundings a bit longer, taking in the beauty and abundant life around me: the buds and blossoms on the trees, the dormant lilies just beginning to push up through the soil, and the daffodils blooming. Squirrels chattered and birds sang. I strolled through the yard, inhaling the sweet spring air and making my way around to the south side of the house.

I stopped at our old chimney. It still stood proud, fashioned from the strong red clay of the region. I envisioned the fireplace on the other side and recalled wonderful childhood memories lying in front of a roaring fire and drinking hot chocolate on Christmas morning. What an idyllic childhood of love and security I'd had, with a mom who was always there to provide love and comfort.

I sat for a while, lost in thought, barely noticing the light touch to the top of my head. But then it happened a second, then a third time. I waved my hand around to shoo away an uninvited honeybee or some other flying insect. As soon as I put my hand back down, I felt another touch to the top of my head, but this time it was a firm pat. I was immediately transported back in time, lying in bed on a school day feeling a gentle pat–pat–pat to the top of my head. It had been Mom's way of waking me in the morning.

I quickly jumped to my feet and was engulfed in a fragrant cloud of Evening In Paris perfume! The bright, feminine smell of my mom's favorite perfume assured me her essence was with me.

Even though my parents had passed beyond the world of form, they opened a door to a powerful modality they knew I would recognize forging a meaningful connection with fragrant reminders of their love.

*Pamela Nance*

# WHEN YOU'RE DEAD, YOU'RE DEAD

hree months before my mother died, she started seeing dead people.

"Your father showed up last night," she told me. "He was standing by the bedroom doorway."

By then, my dad had been dead for more than a decade. "What did he look like?" I asked.

"Do I need to tell you what your father looked like?" she said in exasperation. But then she stopped for a moment and thought about it. "I guess his hair was darker and he had more of it," she chuckled.

My father had been a beloved physician who had a loving heart. But he was a man of science who did not believe in ghosts.

"When you're dead, you're dead," he would have said. And my mother would have agreed.

But as their daughter, and as a psychologist, my mother's apparitions touched upon my deepest and most far-reaching fascination. That night, I barraged her with questions.

"Were you asleep when he appeared? Did he say anything?" and "How often does he show up?"

Annoyed by my cross-examination, my mother took in a deep, audible breath. "I can assure you; I was wide awake. He appears every few days. Please don't go psychoanalyzing me!" she said. "Now let's see what's on TV."

My wise, intelligent, ninety-eight-year-old mother was clear-minded until the end. But after a week in the hospital and a hodgepodge of failing organs, my partner and I decided to bring her home with hospice. As a physician and a woman of science, my spouse sparingly administered medications and watched for signs of the imminent end. For the next ten days, it felt like the three of us ceased to exist anywhere but in that bedroom.

My mother spoke of her precious memories, her deepest regrets, and the people who had shaped her life. As a non-religious Jew, she had no heaven or hell to wade through and no talk of sin or evil to get in her way. She had never been one to talk about the afterlife at all… until spirits began to enter the room.

"It doesn't matter whether you believe me or not," my mother said. "But I'm telling you, your father was standing in the doorway."

"I believe you."

In the last few days, it was as if my mother had one foot in each world. She spoke coherently to me but also continued her conversations with her dead husband and son. Even her bridge partner of seventy years, the most recent of her loved ones to die, showed up at the foot of her bed.

"Can you believe Janis is here?" she said to me. "But she won't say hello or goodbye."

"You know how Janis is," I commented flippantly. But I held back tears, knowing they'd soon be together.

Invisible beings crowded into the bedroom. I didn't see them, but somehow, I knew they were there. One presence stood out above the rest. She planted herself at my mother's feet as my senses intensified far beyond my thinking. My mind went immediately to the thought of my mother's mother.

I had no conscious memory of my grandmother, who had died the year I was born—yet slowly, her gentle, forceful energy became stronger.

By then, my mother was unable to speak. The hospice nurse said she was actively dying.

"It's ok to go," I whispered, although I didn't mean it. I gently squeezed her hand, our only way of communicating. Her mottled hands and uneven inhalations indicated the end was near. She lay in a deep, coma-like sleep, breathing sporadically.

But then, without warning, she opened her eyes and looked in my direction. As if lit up from within, she whispered my name. "Shar," she said. "My mother is waiting in the next room."

I felt a shock run through me as she reached up to the ceiling with a strength she didn't have. Then her head sank back into the pillow, and she closed her eyes for the last time.

*Sharon Sass*

# KEVIN THE DOG

When I learned my twenty-five-year-old son Kevin had died unexpectedly, I felt as if a trap door had just opened. I was freefalling. Every muscle in my body was clenched trying to hold onto Kevin as if he were in front of me, but it was like trying to hold a cloud.

*Is my life just going to be something to endure?* I thought as the news started to sink in.

"Kev, I need you to let me know you are okay," I whispered. "I will not be okay until I hear from you."

Kevin's childhood had been all about being with friends. His report cards showed comments like "makes friends quickly" and "well-liked by his peers." As a young adult, he would often spend time at music festivals meeting new people and making friends. When asked where he was from, he'd say, "New Hampshire for damn sure!" emphasizing the pseudo-rhyme and his New Hampshire roots.

Kevin referred to Sundays as "Sunday Funday because you get to be lazy all day long." But the day after his funeral was not a Sunday Funday. As I leaned against the kitchen counter for support, I shared with my husband

Tom that I had asked Kevin for a sign to let me know he was okay, but I hadn't heard from him. I wanted Tom to say something comforting, but he just sighed.

"What are we supposed to do now?" I asked.

Tom looked at me with a blank stare. "I don't know."

Every time I allowed myself to think of the future, even if it was just the next day, I panicked. How do you live after your child dies? There were no directions for this. There was no plan. All of it was too big and scary to even think about.

I left the kitchen to grab my hiking shoes and came back to find Tom slumped in a chair at the kitchen table with his face in his hands.

"Let's take the dogs for a walk," I suggested.

Kevin was an avid animal lover and an expert at having fun. He grew up with several beloved Golden Retrievers, and during summer vacations on Lake Winnipesaukee, you would find Kevin swimming with the dogs, leaving the water only long enough to race the dogs down the dock and jump back into the lake. Tom and I joked that Kev got along with animals so well because he shared their sense of fun and lived in the present.

Normally, I don't let my dogs interact with other dogs on our walks. Dog walkers often claimed their dog was friendly, even when the animal's body language said otherwise. But on this day, Tom and I decided we were going to have Kevin's attitude and try to enjoy everything, including fellow walkers and their dogs. On this day, we were going to talk to people on the trails. By doing so, we would attempt to bring Kevin's spirit as close to us as we could.

We parked in the small dirt parking lot of a local conservation area three miles from our house. I opened the door of my truck, grabbed two leashes, and let Manny and Tripp out of their crates. It was early October, so the foliage wasn't quite at its peak yet, but it was sunny and unseasonably warm. The dogs, glad to be back on the trails, got busy catching up on the smells they had missed over the past week.

Tripp was methodically sniffing some pine needles while Manny dropped to have a luxurious roll, his back legs kicking in the air as if he were pedaling a bicycle. Seeing Manny enjoy himself so thoroughly took my mind off my grief and into the moment where, for a few seconds, everything was right again.

Tom and I continued our walk mostly in silence as we watched the dogs explore. A woman had turned onto our trail up ahead and was walking slowly toward us. She was looking at our dogs with a friendly smile on her face.

"What beautiful dogs!" she said. "May I pet them?"

"They would love that," I replied, managing a small smile.

She was petting Tripp when Manny trotted up, holding a ball we had brought with us.

When the woman reached for the ball, I said, "He doesn't want you to throw it. He's just showing it to you. He'll be super happy if you just tell him how awesome you think it is."

She followed my instructions perfectly by putting her hands on her knees and leaning toward him while she said, "What do you have there, Manny?"

Manny responded by whining and wiggling his body with the ball still in his mouth, thrilled to get the attention.

As we parted, she said "Enjoy this beautiful day." Her comment snapped me out of the moment and back to Kevin.

"Same to you," I said softly.

When we were out of earshot, I commented to Tom, "Kev would be happy we are out talking to people."

"I agree," he said, nodding.

We were on the last thirty yards that led back to the parking lot when we spotted a family who had just approached the trail entrance. They were strolling toward us with a very excited, white-and-tan boxer mix who strained at the end of his leash like a sled dog.

I started to anticipate a problem but reminded myself we were trying to be open and friendly—like Kevin. The dog was wagging his tail at us frantically, like he was greeting old friends. Since he didn't seem aggressive, we stopped as the family reached us.

The three dogs were intrigued with each other, tails wagging, sniffing and being sniffed. Tom and the woman were making small talk while I kept an eye on the dogs, making sure their behavior didn't take a turn. The kids stood off to the side letting the dogs have their greeting. Then the boxer mix went down on his elbows and hoisted his butt up in the air to signal a game of chase, and we knew it was time to end our conversation. Three excited dogs zipping around little kids was not a good idea.

We had just turned to leave when we heard the mother say, "Let's go, Kevin."

My breath hitched in my throat. Tom and I turned to look at the woman. We were expecting her to be talking to the little boy, but she was looking at her dog!

The dog was once again pulling at the end of his leash, ignoring her, completely focused on us.

"Come on, Kev," she said, giving a little tug on the leash.

We stood just a few feet away with our mouths agape, looking at this dog who didn't want to leave us.

*Oh my God. This is my sign.*

I glanced back to the mother. "Is your dog's name Kevin?" I asked in disbelief.

"Yes! He's a rescue. He came with the name," she said with a grin. She turned to gather her family and they started to walk away.

Stunned by the enormity of it all, my first thought was, *He answered me.*

I dropped to my knees and sobbed. Hearing my distress, the mother turned and looked at me with concern.

Tom knelt beside me and asked, "Should tell her?"

"Yes!" I said, waving him away.

I called our dogs to lie down beside me so I could try to absorb the magnitude of what was happening. I watched the woman clamp her hand over her mouth as Tom told her our story, which ended in a teary hug.

Tom walked back to me, wiping his wet cheeks as the family hiked around the bend and out of sight. I was still crying, but a slow smile took over.

Walking back to the parking lot, I felt a little lighter. I hoisted the dogs into the truck and closed the door. What was I feeling? A flutter of excitement? Hope?

I shook my head in wonder, but I had my answer.

I heard Kevin on that warm October day. He came through loud and clear, saying, *I'm here, and I'm okay. You can smile, even in your darkest hour.*

*Susan Lynch*

# THE RED STONE

*M*y nephew Ken died suddenly and tragically in the autumn of 2012. He was crossing a New York City street after attending a concert with his girlfriend and two other friends when a truck hit him. He was twenty-six years old.

My sister got the call at 4:30 that morning, the worst day of her life. The heavy weight of grief and shock was impossible to escape for his parents, sister, and family. Many in our community felt it, too. Kenny had so many friends. He was a kind and intelligent soul, wise beyond his years.

My sister's grief was especially intense. No one knew how to help. Each morning, I would meet her, and we'd walk and talk. Each night, I'd go to her house and give Reiki sessions to her, Ken's dad, and sister. I was still new to Reiki then, but I could sense benevolent beings around us all. I could feel Kenny was there, too, assisting somehow. I felt as if he was saying things to me. I wasn't frightened by these communications, but they seemed impossible.

*I'm just imagining it,* I would think. I didn't really know how to convey his words without alarming his loved ones.

Kenny told me about the importance of getting through this time of grief. He said we should "have a brave heart." He also said as a family, we were working on important goals and needed to keep our perspective on the bigger picture.

Eventually, I began to share many of the things he was saying to me. My sister seemed too numb and overwhelmed to receive her late son's messages. I wanted so much to help but realized the best I could do was to simply show up and pray. We had to keep going through this nightmare.

Kenny was buried on his birthday, a week after he passed. Nothing about life was the same. His parents were barely getting through each day. A few days after the funeral, I was outside taking pictures of dragonflies still lingering in the warm October weather. I heard Kenny loud and clear.

*Tell my mom when she finds a red stone, it will be from me.*

The communication was direct and calm, yet it shook me up a bit. I ran home to share the news with my husband. He immediately stopped me from calling my sister.

"If you tell her, she's going to be looking for it. Just wait and see what happens. Don't tell her. Write down what you heard and record the date. I'll be your witness as to what he said."

The next morning, my sister and I walked, as usual. Nothing happened.

The day after that, my sister told me that she had recently found a book on beach stones at a local shop. She said she was drawn to it from the window, and she was excited to tell me because the book was dedicated to a man named Ken. She had bought us each a copy. I wondered if this was what Ken had been speaking of in his message to me, but I still hesitated to tell her.

When I got home, my husband said, "It's a good thing you didn't say anything, because that's not a red stone! It's a book. Be patient."

Two more days passed.

Again, we were on our walk. My sister seemed more cheerful, telling me that Ken's dad was moving his business to the home and creating an office. She said, "He's been cleaning up the old desk up in the attic and way back inside the top drawer, I found the coolest thing!"

"What was it?" I asked. I certainly wasn't thinking of a rock.

"Oh my God, it's the coolest stone you've ever seen!" she gushed. "It's smooth and red, and it has a big circle in the middle of it. When I hold it underwater, it gets even more red!"

I couldn't believe what I was hearing. "That's a sign from Ken," I said.

She took a deep breath, "I kind of felt that it was somehow, but how could I really know?"

She was craving proof that her son was okay. I had to tell her. "Ken spoke to me several days ago and said he was sending you a red stone. I wrote it down!"

After that, my sister had some hope again, something to hold on to. A touchstone, direct from heaven. She kept the stone on her kitchen counter as a treasured gift. Every time I would be there for Reiki, she would place the stone on her heart before we began.

"Brave heart," she would say. "The red is for courage and strength."

*Mary Naraya*

# A HUG FROM HEAVEN

woke up at five a.m. and was aware it was my departed father's birthday. He had always gotten up at five, so that time of the day makes me think of him. I could not go back to sleep, so I decided to sit on the couch and quietly send my Dad some birthday love. I had such a strong desire to have a conversation with him and to express my love for him on his special day.

I took a few deep breaths and asked Dad to be with me and to communicate with me. As I did so, I felt an intense distraction. I kept hearing the name "Tom Crook" loudly in my mind. I acknowledged this and sent him love. Tom had been the older brother of my daughter Hannah's friend. At sixteen years of age, Tom had committed suicide a couple of years earlier.

Now, each time I tried to be in the presence of my Dad, I would hear "Tom Crook."

Finally, I said, "Hey, Dad, I am trying to talk to you but I keep hearing Tom Crook's name. It's so loud, I can't focus."

My Dad responded by saying, *That's because he is right here with me!*

Startled, I said, "Please give Tom a hug!"

To which my Dad replied, *What makes you think I'm not already hugging him?*

"How could that be, Dad?" I asked, puzzled. "You never knew him."

Adopting a sarcastic tone, my late father began to explain. *You are connected with Tom's mother, Becky, so I am connected with Tom. That's how this works.*

"How would I know how it works?" I asked, and I could sense him laughing.

I got excited thinking that I could get a message from Tom to his mother, Becky. At this point, Dad was the only person I had ever felt and communicated with from the other side. I wasn't sure I *could* communicate with anyone else. I asked Dad to help me hear from Tom, so that I could get a message to his mom.

Then I addressed Tom directly. "If it's really you, please give me a message for your mom."

I heard nothing. In fact, I could no longer feel my father's presence. Discouraged, I went back to my bedroom to try to sleep, thinking that it might be easier for Tom to get a message to me if I was asleep.

As I laid my head on my pillow, I mentally asked Tom to send me a message for his mom. Instantly, I saw an image reel in my mind. A young boy with brown hair, wearing a karate outfit, was saying: *You ain't seen nothing, look at this!* He then performed a fancy, round house kick. He was so proud; I could feel his emotions and thoughts. He felt confident and powerful.

That was it. Nothing else came through.

I thought, *Who the heck was that?* I did not recognize that kid. I asked Tom, "What kind of message was that? Please send me another message that makes more sense."

Immediately, I saw a still image of a dark, golden-yellow color with black, vertical stripes. I heard, *Notice how wide the stripes are.*

I was baffled. Neither of these images made any sense. And he was gone.

I knew Tom Crook's mother, Becky, but I didn't have a very close relationship with her. Since these messages didn't make sense to me, I was afraid to mention them, so I did not.

Two or three months later, at a soccer game for our girls, I saw Becky. As she approached me, I could see she was particularly down. When I asked how she was doing, she began to cry.

"I went to the cemetery last night and asked Tom to help me if he could. I told him I desperately needed a hug from him, because life was too hard without him." She sobbed. "I said I didn't know if I could go on."

I realized I needed to tell her. "I think I heard from Tom."

We moved back slightly from the soccer field and sat in a more private spot, away from the noise of the game. It felt like a circle of protective energy surrounded us.

"Becky, something strange happened on my Dad's birthday a couple of months ago. Dad said he was with Tom and was hugging him."

"But your father didn't know Tom!" she said, her voice hushed.

"He explained that they are connected because you and I are connected."

When I told her about the images I had seen, which still made no sense to me, Becky's eyes lit up. "I saw a little brown-haired boy doing a round house kick, wearing a karate outfit."

"That was Tom! He loved that karate class. That was a time when Tom felt great about himself before he started to struggle with depression. I even have a video tape of Tom doing that round house kick. It's one of my favorite memories of him!"

Then, I told her about the image of the dark yellow color with the wide, black, vertical stripes. She said it might have something to do with the stripes on muscle cars. Their family owns several of these old cars.

By this time, the soccer game was over, and Becky wanted to rush home to find the video tape of Tom's karate performance. I offered to take the girls to my house, so she could have some privacy while watching the tape.

About an hour or so later, I got a call from her. "Can you come over right now? I have something to show you."

Becky hadn't been able to find the specific video tape she was looking for, but she did find a video that included a few moments of Tom doing some karate. We watched the tape together. I was sure this was the little boy I had seen in my vision.

The video then went into a Christmas scene where a younger Tom, was opening his gifts. There were lots of presents!

At one point, Tom walked over to Becky and handed her a wrapped gift from him. It was a necklace. Becky expressed how much she loved it and then she opened her arms wide and Tom ran into them and gave her a long, full-bodied hug! This was what Becky had called me over to see.

"Look," she said. "I got the hug I asked Tom for!" She said she had felt it coursing through her body as she watched it.

We were both crying then, overwhelmed that Tom had managed to give his mom a hug from the other side! Suddenly, in the video, we saw Tom running up to hug his dad. Since his father was holding the video camera, all we could see was Tom's pajama top, close to the camera lens.

It was dark golden yellow with wide black stripes! Now we knew this was exactly what he had planned all along.

That day was a turning point for Becky. She told me she felt such relief to know Tom had heard her plea, that he was still "alive" and aware of everything. His message had been a gift beyond measure.

That was the day she realized she could survive her sixteen-year-old son's suicide, because he was still with her—in new ways.

*Melissa Knutson*

# DAD'S HOUSE

hen he was alive, my father and I were not the best of friends. His many years of alcoholism, depression, and volatility kept my sister and me at arm's length and made him increasingly withdrawn. When he passed away in 1987, it was a sad but liberating time for my family. He was free and so were we.

Then, when my own life took some colorful twists and turns, I began to feel I understood my father more, on an emotional and visceral level. I have practiced meditation for many years, and as my practice evolved, I began to wonder, *Is my Dad still here, across the veil—and if he is, could I engage him in conversation?*

Could we still heal the breach that existed between us, from opposite sides of the physical divide?

I signed up for a course to develop my mediumship skills. As the course progressed, I and my fellow students would schedule one-on-one calls with each other, to talk about our lessons and practice. Another student and new friend of mine, Becky, seemed to make a connection with Dad right away. Although she did not know any of my family history, she described him in detail. And then, through Becky, he began to speak.

Dad launched into a series of apologies for his conduct and its detrimental effects on the family. He spoke in such a heart-wrenching way that Becky cried during the reading. I was dumbstruck.

I wrote down the details of the reading she did for me, which included my father expressing a desire to make amends for any hurt he had caused. He also spoke about his desire to help my sister, Melissa, and me find a new home.

Melis and I were living in San Francisco, where we had shared my parents' former home for eighteen years. But both of us really wanted a change from city living. For some months, we had been trying to figure out where we might relocate to a life in the country with open spaces, more serenity, a lower crime rate, and a place to grow vegetables. I started searching real estate listings in Ashland, Oregon for a nice country house that would meet our needs and give us an opportunity for a new life.

In a reading with a mediumship student, my father described the place he saw for us in specific detail. It was a Craftsman-style house on the edge of a steep hill, overlooking the water, with a beautiful view of the mountains. It had lovely trees and a nice front porch. When my reader shared this information with me, I was touched by the thought that my dad was trying to help us—but nothing about the home he described sounded like any listing I had looked at. It didn't even sound like the kind of situation we might find in Ashland, which is three hours from the Oregon coast. So I tabled the information about "Dad's House" for the time being and concentrated on houses that were available.

But Dad was not done with the subject. In three subsequent readings—with students around the country, and even one in Canada—he appeared to my readers and added to the previous description. Each time, I thought how funny it was that all these readings seemed to offer assistance in my home search, but his advice bore no relationship to any houses I had seen over several months.

It wasn't until July of that same year that my sister and I were able to manage a trip up to Ashland, to look at some houses in person. The real estate market was a hot market at that time, and several properties we had been interested in had either been sold or were no longer on the market. One place that we liked was sold to someone else on our first day in town. Only two properties remained for us to view out of my original list of possibilities— and we weren't really excited about either one.

When we visited the last house on a very hot July afternoon, the first thing we noticed was a beautiful, cool breeze blowing through the open windows. The house was on the south end of town and had a big oak tree off the back deck, providing a lot of pleasant shade. Beyond that was open space with the mountains in the distance and that nice breeze, a welcome relief from the heat of downtown.

Walking out to the back deck, we saw a wonderful creek rushing by and heard the lovely sound it was making. As we continued our tour of the house, we noticed one thing after another that we liked. We came back for a second look that day and made a full-price offer to the owners the very next day, which they accepted.

We received an all-cash offer on our house in San Francisco within a week of our return. We were packed up and moved to Ashland by early September, ready to start our new lives.

After getting somewhat settled in, I went on a search for my notes from all those mediumship readings of the previous March. *Was this really the house Dad had in mind for us?* I hadn't realized it when we first saw it, but my notes confirmed that my dad had described every detail of this house in Ashland, five months before we ever set eyes on it.

He had mentioned the Craftsman-style construction and the water view, our wonderful creek as well as the steep hill behind the house and our nice stone porch, where we look out at our spectacular vistas. He had told Becky that he wanted my sister and I to have beautiful views to compensate for his being emotionally absent when he was alive. Well, he couldn't have done better. We have a magnificent view from every room in the house. Even our friends remark about it.

Dad had mentioned that the house was either blue or gray in color. We learned that it was blue at the time it was listed but had been painted light gray by the time we saw it. Dad even said that there was a built-in desk in the office where we could sit and write together. There is. Check, check, check!

Every day, I marvel at the relationship I have today with my beautiful Dad in Spirit. We have gone from being entirely estranged to being dear and special friends. I love him. I was never able to say that before and mean it. The rift between us is healed now, emotionally and spiritually. I find indescribable joy in knowing that he is still out there, with Mom, helping us out and guiding the way. I give thanks every day.

And every morning, when I look out the kitchen window at the beautiful Cascade Mountains, hear the creek rushing through our little ravine, and listen to the birds greeting us with their singing and funny chatter, I think, *Thank you, Dad, for your love, and eternal presence. Today, in a very real sense, our house is your house, too.*

*Annie Brunelli*

# SUNSHINE THROUGH THE RAIN

bolted awake and frantically ran my hands through my hair but found nothing. I had been waking in this manner far too often, each time leaving me more anxious and exhausted.

My heart still pounding, I took a deep breath and slowly expanded my awareness until I sensed the warm, subtle presence of my great-grandmother, Mamita. Mamita had been a calm oasis in a confusing and overwhelming world. When I was a sensitive child, her home was one of the few places I felt completely at ease. She offered me unconditional love and a whole lot of home-grown, homemade, delicious food, in which every bite filled me with love—her love.

Later in her life she was diagnosed with Alzheimer's. It was heartbreaking to watch her slowly fade away. By this time, Mamita was living in the large Victorian house we shared with my grandparents.

One day, my grandmother had to do some errands and left me alone with Mamita. We sat in the kitchen sharing tea. As soon the front door closed, I felt a shift in Mamita. She looked up at me and suddenly her eyes brightened. The light was in her eyes again! She was completely lucid. I sat there, stunned, as she began to tell me stories about her intuition and her experiences with those who had crossed over.

I was about eleven at this time and I'd had similar experiences, but I felt conflicted about this part of my life, even questioning my sanity. Hearing someone I loved and trusted talk about this was not only a breath of fresh air but a lifeline! I tried to soak it all in. Unfortunately, as quickly as this amazing exchange began, it ended. When we heard the front door open, her eyes glazed over. I wanted to scream, "No, Mamita, come back!" but I knew in my heart that the window had closed.

She soon moved to a nursing home and crossed over a few years later, when I was thirteen. Over the following years, in times of stress, I sometimes felt her presence, but this hadn't happened in quite a long time. Now we were experiencing some scary financial issues. *Could I be hearing from Mamita in my dreams, thirty-four years after her death?* Perhaps it was just my imagination.

Acknowledging that my restless doubt was moving toward warp speed, I quietly got up and went downstairs to the living room. Curling up on the sofa, I realized how tired I was. I was wide awake physically, but mentally and spiritually, I felt lost.

Memories of Mamita's funeral began to flash through my mind. My mom had let me attend the mass and burial with a friend of the family. It was a rainy day, but when the hearse turned into the cemetery, the rain had stopped. Honestly, it had rained so much that we weren't prepared for what happened next. The sun began to peek through the clouds, and by the time Mamita's coffin was placed next to where her beloved husband was buried, the clouds had parted just overhead. Beautiful light streamed down, filling my heart with the awe of this sacred moment. The sun gave me a sense that Mamita was saying goodbye and telling us she was happy. I felt her love and warmth. As soon as the service was over, the clouds gathered, and soon the rain returned. I stood there as the gentle raindrops fell.

But was it real? Or was it just my sorrow interpreting things to soothe my pain? Was my sensing Mamita's presence earlier, after my frightened awakening, just wishful thinking?

Once again, I felt the familiar presence. It was time to stop running and engage.

"Hi, Mamita," I whispered aloud. "Please help me. I'm trying to understand this and, well, frankly, I'm trying to believe it's real. I mean, are you touching my hair? If it is you, why? And I need proof—something I can't just push aside. I know I'm asking a lot, but I'm lost and confused. I need a sign, something real to hold onto.

"Mamita, let's be honest—part of me just wants it all to stop. Yet … my heart wants it to be you. If I knew you were here, I'd feel safe with all the uncertainty we're dealing with financially. Please, Mamita. Help me."

The tears streamed down my face. I wiped them away and felt Mamita smile, her warmth surrounding me as I made my way back upstairs to bed.

The next few days felt lighter somehow. Perhaps crying and describing my fears aloud had been cathartic. One night, I was particularly tired and fell into a very sound sleep. The next morning, I felt so refreshed! I was surprised when my usually easy-going husband, Paul, was grumpy and seemed completely out of sorts.

I asked what was wrong and he said he had not slept well. "During the night, I woke up and saw an older woman standing over you, touching your hair. I was still half asleep and I worried this woman would hurt you. I was about to get out of bed when our eyes met. The woman smiled and disappeared."

I felt electric excitement run through my body! I peppered Paul with questions about what she looked like. Finally, I ran upstairs to find a picture I had of Mamita. "Yes," he said. "That could be her. Who is she?"

I reminded him about my great-grandmother and her importance in my life.

While Paul is deeply spiritual, he's also very solid and grounded. I believe Mamita knew that if she came through to Paul and he confirmed it, I would trust his vision more than if I had experienced it myself. This was the proof I had been looking for!

After showering, I went into our bedroom to meditate. I was still buzzing with excitement. Again, I felt her graceful presence. "It's you! It's really you," I said. "I've missed you. You taught me so much. Oh Mamita, how I remember your cooking. What I wouldn't give to taste your sauce one more time!" As soon as I said it, I began to smell a familiar aroma. Suddenly, my mouth was filled with the taste of Mamita's sauce. It was just as I remembered—but it was the love I felt that completely overwhelmed me.

The next day, my parents came over for the weekend. I couldn't wait to tell my mom. She and Mamita had been extremely close. Once we were alone, I shared my experiences of waking up in the middle of the night and Paul's recent experiences meeting Mamita. "I even tasted Mamita's sauce one more time!"

I noticed my mother's eyes were misty. We were quiet for a moment and then she said, "Mamita used to stroke my hair all the time." I again sensed Mamita's presence and sent her my heartfelt gratitude.

My mom and I spent a happy afternoon reminiscing and sharing our love for a woman who had made such a difference in each of our lives.

*Marie Scivetti*

# EXCUSE THE MESS

My hand trembled as I took the door key out of my creased jacket pocket and clumsily thrust it into the lock. I felt a wave of strong emotion, grief mixed with nausea. Tears clouded my eyes. This was the first time I'd been back to the house, my childhood home, since Mum had died, only a month earlier.

A waft of slightly musty, old air hit my nostrils. Gone were the aromas of home cooking, coffee brewing, and Mr. Sheen furniture polish. Gone, too, was the cheery, sing-song voice of my mum ushering me in, tightly hugging me and asking if I would like a cup of tea after my long journey from the South of France to Nottingham, United Kingdom.

Memories of previous visits floated up to the surface my mind: unpacking my suitcase and producing French cheeses, specialty crackers, and fresh asparagus and strawberries, much to the delight of my parents. Mum used to joke and say I'd brought a portable French supermarket with me.

But now my suitcase contained just a few necessities, and the house was eerily vacant of bustling life and warm welcomes. I slowly closed the front door, and alone in the hallway, I collapsed onto the stairs. Overcome with sadness, I sobbed.

The truth was, I had come to empty my parent's house of all their worldly goods. My parents had been married for sixty years, and my father had passed on a year ago, then my mother, a short six months later.

I sensed Mum had died of a broken heart, going into cardiac arrest an hour before her scheduled surgery for an aortic valve replacement. My brother and I were by her side. I was holding her hand, softly speaking to her, telling her how much I loved her and that it was fine for her to go. I felt her soul gently slip away.

Clearing out the house was not a simple task. The grief of losing both my parents in a short space of time and facing the amount of stuff they'd accumulated over the years overwhelmed me. They owned books on every subject known to man and boxes and stacks of photographs. Their closets were bursting with garments, boots, and shoes. I would need to sort through art, kitchenware, gadgets, tools, old crockery ... the list seemed endless.

Amid all this chaos, I felt disheartened and weepy as I tried to organize items into piles, with the intention of finding them new homes. A trip to the nearby thrift store popped up in my thoughts; *Yes, the clothes, shoes, and books would undoubtedly have the opportunity of a second life there.*

I sat in the living room and slowly sifted through various objects. Some held more memories than others. I recalled their origins, where they were displayed, and the precious meaning they held for my parents, myself, and my siblings. I almost felt physically attached to some of the objects because of the nostalgic sentiments. One pile, the things I felt I had to keep close to me at all costs, grew exponentially. By now, the living room floor was covered with boxes and bags, their contents spilling over, creating an untidy and odd assortment of bric-a-brac.

Finally, I mustered the courage to emotionally remove my illogical attachment to my father's leather, lace-up brogues. I managed to let go of my mother's floral dresses, slippers, and twin sets. The books and ordnance survey maps of every square mile of Great Britain could go. Everything I could part with filled five cartons, which I loaded into the car, bound for the local thrift store.

The Sue Ryder Charity Shop was on a busy street and the nearest parking was a five-minute walk away. This did not dampen my enthusiasm for completing this donation. However, once parked, I realized that I would have to make several journeys, carrying one heavy carton at a time. With no alternative, I set out to do it.

A young, chatty sales assistant helped me drag each carton inside, stacking them near the checkout counter. As I delivered the last box, a wave of relief swept over me, and I took a moment to get my breath back. Out of the corner of my eye, I noticed an unusual display of kitschy household objects on a small table, each with a blue raffle ticket stuck to it. Beneath the table was a large bucket with a sea of blue tickets inside.

The display was part of a raffle of items—*probably old stock or junk they couldn't sell*, I thought, as I perused the small animal ornaments, toilet roll holder dolls, tiny plastic cacti in pots, and faded Christmas decorations amongst other things.

Overcome by a strange urge to have a go, I dropped some money in the donation box on the table. I plunged my hand into the bucket, picked out a blue ticket, and gave it to the young assistant. She smiled as she handed me the item which had the corresponding ticket number on it.

A surge of electricity zapped through my body. The hair on my arms stood to attention, pricked by goosebumps. I was bowled over by what she handed me: a small, white, wooden plaque with black italic writing that read: "EXCUSE the mess, but we just wanted you to feel at home."

I instinctively clutched the plaque to my heart, thanked the assistant, and dashed away from the store. I knew this was a message, a sign from Mum and Dad. The sense of humor of this phrase was perfectly suited to how they were when they were alive, and the message was perfect for the current situation.

Tears came, this time joyful ones, accompanied by a warm, tingling feeling of love.

They were with me. No other explanation.

*Elizabeth Clark*

# TAKING HIS FINAL FLIGHT HOME

*W*hen I got the call that my stepdad had passed away at the assisted living facility, I rushed across town to take care of the necessary details. At ninety-one years of age, he'd lived an adventurous and honorable life.

James Todd, my stepfather, was a Navy pilot in World War II. When they decommissioned pilots at the end of the war, he re-enlisted in the Marines to continue flying. His group was known as "The Flying Peons." He was twice decorated with a Distinguished Flying Cross, and by the time he retired in 1969, he'd saved the lives of thirty-six Marines during a fierce battle in Vietnam. He was a tough old bird and did not suffer fools.

He and I had a troubled relationship in my youth. It was difficult to have a stepfather, and we often had intense disagreements. However, in the mid-1980s, he gave me my first command: "Promise me that you'll look out for me during my last days." I felt it was an order from a tough old Marine to a sometimes-rebellious kid.

Being his advocate during the most stressful time of his life was not easy. It was particularly hard to order around a Marine who had once ordered around General Westmoreland! Yet he had put his life in my hands, and it became a spiritual privilege and challenge to help him. As a man of honor and integrity, he always kept his promises. It was my honor to keep my promise to him.

Over the year that he was in assisted living, I noticed his heart softening toward me. He developed a lovely humility as he contemplated his life and impending transition. He didn't like it when I had to tell him no regarding issues that might endanger him or were not in his best interest, but he eventually understood that the choices I made for his well-being were made with love.

An old family friend who visited him two days before he died said to me, "Wow, your dad was such an S. O. B. (Stern, Obstinate, Bloke), but now... he's a lamb!"

When I got the call that he had passed away, I rushed across town to take care of the necessary details. After his body was removed from the facility, I walked outside and immediately felt an intense rush of powerful and loving energy surround me, and then a heartfelt 'thank you' bear hug! As I looked toward the Catalina Mountains north of Tucson, AZ, I could see his spirit fly a maneuver, a fly-by, in front of the mountains. Then, he sped away, free from the encumbrance of his body, disappearing at lightning speed.

Driving home I turned on my radio and it immediately played Natalie Merchant's song, "Kind and Generous." It struck me that this was his way of thanking me for caring for him. Later that night, I listened to a classical music playlist on my phone that my son had recommended a few months prior. Something was compelling about the piece that the cellist was playing, and I felt prompted to pay closer attention and to look at the playlist. The song was titled *Esperance*. My last name is Esparza, and *espérance* is French for *hope*.

I burst into happy tears when I saw that the musician's name was James Todd! There it was, *my stepfather's name* as the musician playing a lovely song of hope, letting me know that he was alive and near.

*Melinda Esparza*

# UPSIDE-DOWN AND PERFECT

*A*fter our son Dakota died, my wife became a voracious reader. Most of Gloria's reading focused on spirituality, near-death experiences (NDEs), and the reality of life after death. We were both desperately looking for some sort of proof that our son was both happy on the other side and yet somehow still with us.

Gloria scoured the internet for teachings that would bring us peace, and soon our home started filling up with books written by people who had lived through circumstances very similar to ours. She would find the best parts of each book and either read them to me or dog-ear the pages so that I could read them later. These books gave us comfort, especially on the toughest days after losing Dakota.

Like millions of people, she buys most of her books through Amazon, since we don't live near any bookstores. One morning, she opened her Amazon account and saw that, for some reason, she had one item in her cart. She thought that was odd, since she hadn't left anything in there the last time she'd been online. *Very odd.*

Curious, she clicked on the cart icon and saw that *Still Right Here* by Suzanne Giesemann was ready for checkout. Gloria had no idea how the book had gotten into her cart but, after reading the description and the reviews, she eagerly and happily ordered it.

When the book arrived a few days later, she almost ran to the front porch where the Amazon driver had left it. She brought it inside and, with the enthusiasm of a kid at Christmas, ripped the package open and snagged the book. Then she opened it up to the first page and cried, "What the hell?"

She repeated that phrase several more times with increasing anger as she kept flipping the pages. I walked over and saw the source of her confusion: The first 138 pages of the book had been printed upside-down!

Being the "fixer" that I am, I whipped open my Mac, found a couple email addresses associated with the author, and fired off some not-so-polite emails. We were hoping to get a book that would bring us comfort and much-sought-after peace, I wrote—and, who knows, even a little bit of happiness. Instead, we got a book that was, in my opinion, completely useless. I even questioned their production process and sent along a little video of the upside-down book.

Imagine my surprise when I got an email back almost immediately from the author's scheduler Lynette, then another one from her staffer Bev and—the biggest shock of all—one from Suzanne Giesemann herself. All were very apologetic. All of them said they had never had something like this ever happen before.

But what blew our minds were the questions Suzanne asked and the comments she made. She asked, "Was Dakota a bit of a prankster? Did he like a good joke? Did he have an unusual way of looking at the world? I have seen those across the veil pull off some amazing things to get people's attention, and the ways they do it often relate to things in their life."

Suzanne sent that note at the exact moment that Gloria and I were having the same discussion. Dakota had been sending us signs that he was still watching over us ever since he had transitioned. To say that our son had an unusual way of looking at the world would be quite an understatement.

He had an IQ of 155 but was saddled with lots of learning differences. He had acute attention-deficit problems as well as sensory dysfunction and dyslexia. Throughout his twenty-three years, he developed a reputation for his wicked sense of humor, his amazing guitar playing, and his unique and extremely creative way of looking at the world.

As a dear friend once said, "I love the way Dakota's brain works. And I love the fact that it is rarely where his body is."

Our boy saw the world through a unique lens that was full of passion, curiosity, and humor. Dakota's beautiful, loving and kind spirit drew all sorts of people to him. And because of that, when his life ended in 2021, he was being prayed for by musicians, artists, athletes, lawyers, farmers, business leaders, Native Americans, African Americans, Hindus, Christians, rabbis and even a retired major general. Everybody loved Dakota. He didn't just live life—he devoured it.

His love for humor was paramount in his life here on Earth. We spent many hours watching comedy together on YouTube and he was always searching for the latest and greatest standup comedians and sketch comedy groups. Starting in middle school, Dakota and his best friend Nolan made some of the oddest, most hilarious videos I've ever seen. In fact, one funny video won Best Student Film in his freshman year of high school.

Did our son Dakota see the world from a unique perspective? Absolutely.

Would he think it would be funny to send us a book that was printed upside down? Oh, yeah.

Do we believe that Dakota somehow managed to make it happen? Without a doubt.

We treasure the book now and see it as a not-so-subtle reminder that Dakota is, as Suzanne Giesemann would say, *still right here.*

*Jim Spruell*

# THE JOURNAL

*A*t my son's Jason Celebration of Life, the turnout was much more than I expected. I was touched at how many people showed up, knowing that many of them also struggled with addiction, and I understood the deep pain that comes with it. Some of those who attended had been in rehab with Jason several times, and a few caring counselors came as well. The theme was beautifully redundant as they shared stories of his kindness and compassion, the way he always took care of everyone else but struggled with doing this for himself.

One of Jason's friends who showed up was named David. I'd never met him before, but I immediately sensed his love for Jason and felt the essence of his caring soul. A few weeks later, David and I started to talk on social media, since I lived in Florida and he was in California. We became close over the next few months. We were on the same spiritual journey, which made our relationship grow even stronger.

David and I often shared our many visits from Jason, and I was thankful, as this became a big part of my healing in the early months. We mostly texted or messaged each other, but one day he decided to call me. He told me he was excited that he was going to see a medium and would let me know if Jason came through.

A few weeks later—around seven months after Jason transitioned—David told me Jason had come through, but he was a little bewildered by the main message he'd sent. The medium said that Jason told her that David needed to "give Mom the book." I was just as confused about what this meant, but being an optimist, I said, "Well, maybe it will make more sense later."

Another month passed, and David called me again. "I know what book I am supposed to give you."

I was so excited. "What is it?"

"I'm going to have to tell you when I see you in person. It's a crazy story," he replied.

I was flying to California in a few weeks, and we planned to meet for lunch at the Mission Inn, which had been one of Jason's favorite places to take photographs. We both felt like Jason chose the Mission because it is a historical landmark and a spiritual, tranquil setting. We'd only met once before, at the celebration of Jason's life, and I think my son was also eager for us to meet in person. And finally, David could tell me the story about "the book."

The day arrived and we enjoyed a wonderful lunch outside. We noticed there was a specific bird that sat nearby the entire time and just stared at us. While the other birds were eating crumbs at nearby tables, this one bird didn't move. David and I both looked at each other and said, "Jason."

Finally, the moment had come to share the mystery of the book. David said he had been walking in an area of town where a few familiar homeless people hang out. One of them had his shoes in his hand and asked David, "Can you give me twenty dollars for my shoes?"

David handed him a twenty-dollar bill and told him to keep the shoes.

The homeless man was grateful. "Well, if you won't take my shoes, at least grab a couple of these books," he told David, pointing to a pile of used paperbacks.

David said he grabbed three random books without really looking at them and hurried away. Later, when he was home, he decided to look at them. One of the books was ragged and looked like it had been singed in a fire. He opened the book and on the first page was written: "This journal belongs to Jason Jardine."

My son.

David was astonished. "I couldn't believe my eyes! I now knew this was the book Jason wanted me to give you—but how and why did this homeless man have Jason's journal? I had to find out."

David went back to the area to find the man. "How did you get my friend's journal?" he demanded.

The homeless man was a bit intimidated and admitted, "I am sorry. I was squatting at this house that burned down, and the book was just lying on the ground, so I picked it up."

The house was on the other side of town and not where he normally hung out. "I knew his story was true because, a few months before Jason transitioned, he had been staying at another friend's house. They'd had a fire and the house almost burned to the ground.

David pulled out Jason's journal and handed it to me. Jason's beautiful, semi-burnt journal was now my treasure!

The drive back to my daughter's house, where I was staying, was a long fifty minutes. I wanted so badly to read my son's words, but I decided to wait until I got back and share it with my daughter as well. This journal was special; it was one that they used in his 12-Step program, and he had filled it with his deepest feelings about his life and struggles. There was so much love and forgiveness on every page.

Jason and I had always had a special connection, as I was a single mom when he was growing up. It was only Jason and me for many years. Now I could read, in his own words, that he felt I was always there for him.

It was a blessing to be able to read the journal and feel the love in his heart. Thank you, my son, for the gift.

*Saundra Gattie*

# NATURE'S WAY OPEN

*H*ave you ever traced with your eyes the fall of a leaf through the autumn air, admiring the beauty and wondering just how long the wind would carry it, this way and that, before it inevitably falls to its new home?

Ten days before my dad's passing, we took a photo together under a gorgeous, full, yellow maple tree. I knew his life was soon ending. My hand rested on his heart as we stared into each other's eyes, silently recognizing a shared lifetime of a sometimes complicated relationship. I smiled, burying the tears that welled up in my heart. Everything was suddenly so simple. I just loved my perfectly, imperfect dad.

During one of our last, mostly lucid conversations, I asked for Dad to send me a signal, so I'd know he was well in his new "home." I pushed through my nerves to be vulnerable and ask for the sign I needed. Dad hadn't wanted to talk at all about dying.

"How about a leaf in my face, Dad?"

He grunted in disapproval of my suggestion.

"Everything will be near. You'll know in the eyes," my dad said.

"I don't know what exactly is possible, Dad, but I believe in possibilities," I said. I closed my eyes and lay back in the chair, thankful for having listened to my heart's nudge.

Days later, my dad entered the state of final transition and hadn't uttered a sound for twenty-four hours. It seemed unimaginable that I'd never again hear his strong, soothing voice. A few days earlier, he'd brought comfort to my heart as he sang me a few bars of a childhood song. Keeping vigil at his bedside, I tried to be perfectly prepared for an event that, like birth, is its own miracle and can only be supported, not controlled.

Lying alongside Dad in his hospice bed, my head on his chest and his warm hand in mine, I surrendered myself to nature's way, like a leaf surrenders to the wind. This journey was my dad's to take, and I needed to learn to let him go. In that stillness, I detached from all the what-ifs, disappointments, and grief, and instead put my power into full presence and unconditional love.

In that moment of surrender, I experienced what I describe as "not of me." As we lay peacefully, hands entwined, I suddenly witnessed swirls of purple in my mind's vision and felt an incredible warmth encompassing my body. I thought the sun from the window must be playing tricks on me. But then with full clarity, I felt an energy enter my back and go into my heart center and swirl around, before moving to my shoulder. From that point, I followed the feeling as it if were a lightning bug as it traveled slowly down my arm, into my hand, and finally—I just knew with total certainty—into my dad.

I hugged him tight and whispered in his ear, "Dad, I don't know what that was, but I hope you felt it too. Take all that love and light in your core with you and leave the old news behind."

I knew, deep within my soul, my dad and I were eternally bonded. I never imagined it possible to feel such peace at such a painful time. At four a.m., with me curled beside him and his hand in mine, my father took his final breath. I had accompanied him on his journey as far as God would allow.

Following his death, I learned that—like the leaf that is no longer on the tree but remains in the world—my dad was not gone at all. This was true not because I wished it to be so, but because his energy remained, and I could feel, hear, and sometimes even engage with his spirit.

I didn't trust this voice at first, but my otherworldly experiences with him grew, accompanied by information I could have never known. I experienced signs and synchronicities without any other possible explanation. My father's after-life presence shook me from my sense of logic, stability, and control. During the next months, he led me through a transformation toward my inner light.

With this awareness, I see with new eyes and have a new sense of being. What once was a pleasurable walk in the woods I can now experience as a joyous state of union with life. Hanging Christmas decorations with family transformed from a fun, seasonal activity to an experience of genuine joy and hope. I am learning to become aware of what arises within when I surrender to his presence in my daily life, meditation, and relationships.

My father's passing carried me through a season of the death of my ego and rebirth of my spirit. I have been graced with an understanding of the beauty and love of a greater reality. I can glimpse the connectedness of us all.

When my dad was led home, my soul opened. Nature's way is beautiful.

*Amber Kasic*

# THE TURTLE

ad experienced some health issues over the summer, but nothing I considered life-threatening—and nothing he seemed to take very seriously. When he went into the hospital that October day, I expected him to be in and out soon, none the worse for wear. We couldn't guess that a perfect storm of medical maladies would conspire to keep him in that hospital bed, as we stood helplessly by.

As he continued to decline in the hospital, Dad had a series of strokes that made communication difficult. But I often felt like I was communicating with him in my dream state and tapping into his inner world. Sometimes, I would wake up with a word in my mind that would later prove meaningful. I even dreamed of song lyrics that provided comfort or answered critical questions.

One night in early December, I dreamt the word "sepsis." It became etched into my consciousness. At the time, I was not familiar with this word, but I knew it had something to do with my father. When I researched the term, I learned that sepsis can be a life-threatening illness.

The doctors assured us that my father did not have sepsis, but a month later, that word would appear on his death certificate.

As the year ended, it became clear that Dad was on his way to his heavenly home. In fact, at one point, he told my mom: "I'm going on home now. You come along when you're ready."

After a particularly rough weekend when Dad pulled his feeding tube out, he seemed to be approaching a crossroads. The doctors had done all they could do. Our family had some difficult discussions about when it might be time to stop prolonging his discomfort.

The next morning, I woke up with Lady Gaga's song "Do What You Want With My Body" in my head. Of course, in the medical context, this song takes on an entirely different meaning. I felt that Dad was communicating with me, saying that anything we decided about his body would be fine with him.

A few weeks before he died, I dreamed a simple but strong image: the white rabbit from Alice in Wonderland. The message was implied, but clear: "I'm late, I'm late for a very important date." I could not shake the feeling that the image was related to Dad. He was struggling to let go.

I have long found guidance, comfort, and inspiration in my dreams. And as a student of shamanism, I hoped to connect with a spiritual guide or power animal who could help Dad make this final transition. Before falling asleep one chilly night in early January, I set the intention to connect with my father's spirit.

In my dreams, I encountered my father as a boy of about ten or twelve. I noticed a small totem on the ground and thought, *He must have dropped this.* It was a turtle made of wood.

I picked it up, handed it to him, saying, "I think this is yours."

Dad gladly took the little figure from me and told me something strange: That to honor the turtle, he would make a turtle costume that he would wear at some kind of important ceremony taking place that night.

Dad died the next day. His passing left a void in our little family that would never be filled. But alongside the grief was comfort in knowing that his life continues beyond the veil, and so does our relationship.

I later learned that the turtle, which carries its home on its back, can signify a long physical or spiritual journey, as well as Divine timing. I shared this dream with no one, but for me, the turtle became a symbol of Dad.

Several years later, on a bright June day, my older sister Paige showed up on my doorstep with a large turtle that seemed to have lost its way and was at risk of getting hit by a car. We safely relocated the turtle to the local park, and I savored the unmistakable sign from Dad.

It was no small thing that the turtle arrived at my door on Father's Day.

*Celeste Huttes*

# SPIRIT GUIDED GPS

I was on my way to pick up some dog food from a store where I had shopped several times already, but since I was new to the area, I was using my GPS to make sure I didn't get lost. As I crossed a major intersection, I thought to myself, *I think that is where I'd usually turn.* I wondered why the GPS hadn't told me to turn there.

After a few more intersections, I became sure that I was not being guided correctly. I decided to pull into the next parking lot entrance so I could turn around and get back to where I should've turned.

As soon as I pulled into the lot, I saw a thrift store called "The Discovery Shop," and my intuition told me to go inside. Even though I don't really enjoy shopping, I knew to listen to my inner guidance—especially considering the name of the store. So, in I went.

As soon as I stepped through the door, I was astounded to see tables full of owl jewelry. Not a mix of different subject matter, just owls upon owls. It was mesmerizing and brought a tear to my eyes. I realized the reason my GPS had misguided me: My sweet dog, Lovey, had commandeered the system and directed me to where he wanted me to be.

A short time earlier, Lovey had made his transition to the spirit world. Only about six hours transpired from the beginning of his medical emergency to his last breath. While his unexpected death was heartbreaking and shocking, it was also an honor to be there with him during such a momentous life event and to witness what happened right before he was euthanized.

I was about to create a healing oasis of light in the examining room, hoping that the vet would have good news when she returned. But before I could do so, a vertical portal of golden light appeared right beside me and Lovey. Another one of my dogs, Astrud, appeared. Astrud is also in the spirit world; she had been Lovey's buddy and had transitioned about ten years earlier.

Now Astrud was there in all her glory, to shepherd Lovey back home.

I knew then that the vet would recommend euthanasia. When she did, I gave permission. My sweet Lovey made his way back home with my hands and forehead, as well as a dear friend's hands, lovingly placed upon him. Once the procedure was complete, the portal closed back up.

As I stood by his grave after burying his little body, I asked my sweet Lovey, "What shall I look for in the coming days? How will you remind me that you are still with me, and just as feisty and funny as ever?"

And just then, an owl hooted. Through my tears, I laughed and asked, "Owls? Will that be our thing from now on?"

Another hoot was heard, which was the confirmation that Lovey was already easy to communicate with.

Not long after his transition, I asked Lovey to "dazzle me today, remind me of your sense of humor." Shortly after this request, I started hearing a buzzing sound and couldn't figure out where it was coming from. I walked through my house trying to locate the sound. When I finally figured out where it was coming from, I said out loud, "Lovey, you really are great at communicating and still have that sense of humor!"

He had guided a fly into a very small opening at the base of a twelve-inch tall, hollow glass owl sitting on my mantle. The opening was there because the statue was chipped. Once the fly was inside, it couldn't get out and started flying around making quite the racket. I took the owl outside and released the fly. Never before, and never since, has a fly ended up inside the owl.

I was again inspired to go to a local thrift store and was drawn to a wall of purses and bags. I carry only a small purse and have no need to buy another one, so I knew I was being guided and would find something meaningful. Front and center hanging on the wall was a handmade bag. The fabric was adorned with paw prints of different colors, and on the small pocket on the front, enveloped by paw prints, was the image of an owl. *Paw prints and an owl.* I silently thanked Lovey, took a photo, and marveled at his skillfulness at multidimensional communication.

Thankfully, I have no doubt that Lovey is still with me, communicating with me every day. And on the days when I need a little boost of joy, or I am feeling his physical absence strongly, he makes sure that I see something fantastic having to do with owls. I believe they are reminders from him that life continues beyond this physical life and our loved ones who have gone on before are still among us—and they sometimes use GPS to guide us to that truth.

*Chenée Fournier*

# MOTHER'S DAY

The greatest joy, purpose, and calling in my life has been the role of mother to my two sons, even though they are no longer here in physical form.

On May 8, 2013, my oldest son Dylan died from a drug overdose. At age twenty-five, he had been sober for some time, but a friend he used to party with had tempted him to get high "for old times' sake." The sudden passing of this bright, beautiful, wise, compassionate young man felt unreal and impossible.

The date of his death was the same as the date my father died in 1979. Dylan's funeral was on Mother's Day.

My younger son Tyson, age twenty-three, struggled to deal with his beloved brother's death. He felt that life was meaningless and would be unbearable without Dylan. He was hospitalized to treat his suicidality. But in June of 2014, shortly after his release and slightly more than a year after Dylan's passing, he succeeded in ending his life.

After losing them both, I did not imagine that I could survive for long. Indeed, I had little wish to live.

In between my sons' deaths, my mother had died. On the first Mother's Day after all these losses—without my mother, without my sons—the pain was indescribable. All holidays are difficult now, but Mother's Day is always the most challenging.

However, Mother's Day in 2021 was special, because of a series of events that I believe were carefully orchestrated by Dylan and Tyson.

It started like another sad holiday. I felt lost and lonely, overwhelmed by the grief welling up inside of me. The day crawled by painfully, and I just prayed for it to be over.

Late that afternoon, I received a text from a local florist. The florist said they could not get into my apartment building to make a delivery. I was close by on a walk and I hurried back to greet the delivery person, who had a magnificent floral arrangement of white, orange, and pink roses along with some purple flowers (my favorite color).

As I received this spectacular arrangement, my mind raced with questions. Who might have sent these flowers to me? The delivery woman then proffered a small gift bag, saying, "They wanted you to have this, too."

I looked inside and the bag contained my favorite type of scented candle. I opened the card and read these words: "Happy Mother's Day, Mom. We love you. Love, Dylan and Tyson."

My jaw dropped and my eyes filled with tears. In shock, I quickly shared my story with the delivery woman, and I saw her eyes tearing up as well. She shared with me that her brother had taken his own life just three weeks earlier. We cried and hugged until she said she had to go and make the rest of her deliveries.

I was stunned by what had just happened and began my search to find out who had sent me the flowers. Did someone who loved me think this would be a beautiful gesture? I contacted all the boys' friends and all my close friends and relatives as well. No one could tell me who sent the flowers, although some said, "What a great idea! I wish I thought of that!"

My next step was to call the florist, thinking there might be a paper trail via a credit card or some type of clue. The woman who answered the phone was the person who takes all the orders, some over the phone, some by people who come into the shop in person. She said there was no credit card receipt, but that she remembered the exact scenario regarding my flowers.

She recalled that two strikingly tall and gorgeous young men had come into the store, one with blue eyes and blonde hair, the other with blue eyes and dark hair. Tyson was six-foot-three with blonde hair and blue eyes; Dylan was the same height with blue eyes and dark brown hair. The florist said these young men had walked into the store, carefully picked out the flowers they wanted to send and dictated the message to appear on the accompanying card. Before they left, they added the candle and gift bag, asking that these be delivered along with the flowers and card. They paid for everything in cash and quietly left the store.

My head spun as I absorbed the florist's account. This was pure, solid confirmation that Dylan and Tyson were reaching out to me across the veil, contacting me in such a unique, meaningful, and loving way. My two indigo angels had stepped out of their realm and into mine to give me comfort, hope, and the highest vibrational energy a mother could ask for!

*Ann Michele*

# LOVE FROM THE OTHER SIDE

*H*ours after my husband died, I sat on my back deck trying to comprehend what had just happened. I could not wrap my head around the harsh truth that he was gone—no longer of this Earth. One minute, he'd been lying in the hospital bed, hooked up to an oxygen source, struggling to breathe. The next minute—gone.

No breath. No life. A motionless body left behind.

Was I aware of his transition? A change in the air, a quickening sort of vibration like a thousand angel wings stirring the air had me on high alert. I looked to my husband for guidance and watched helplessly as his chest heaving and legs shaking he worked at shedding his body.

Ripples in the air continued, echoing the breathing of a body growing tired. The rhythm had changed to a shallow, quicker pace, as if he was wanting to accelerate the process, wanting to get on with this sacred journey.

*What could I do?* My brain was frozen. It came up with nothing. Reality had shifted and I felt like we were being swept along with this invisible force, like a river flowing to the ocean. The ending was inevitable. He was dying, but I could not accept it.

"Please don't go, sweetheart," I cried softly, tears beginning to flow down my cheeks. "Please don't leave this world."

I knew in my heart I shouldn't be saying this. I should be encouraging him to leave, to go in peace and with love, to have a safe passage. But I couldn't do that. I didn't want him to go.

"I love you, sweetheart."

A shallow breath, two, three, then nothing. He was gone and I knew we would never have this moment again, this moment as life crosses over into death.

I don't know how I made my way home. I was in a fog of shock as I unlocked the front door and walked into the empty house. *Where was my husband? Why is he not here in our home?*

Not knowing what else to do, I stepped out the back door and sagged into my garden chair. I had no idea what time it was, nor did I care. *Was my husband really gone? How could he not be here sitting beside me?*

Beautiful shades of orange and gold shimmered over the sky as the day faded and the light began to change. I watched the sunset as if from a great distance, yet I felt a connection in some part of my being, as though I was slowly sinking along with the sun.

Closing my eyes, I sat in the quiet stillness of a soft summer evening. Birds were silent, except for the occasional swishing sound that I thought might be a hummingbird at the feeder. I opened my eyes to look, but the feeder wasn't even there. I hadn't thought to hang it up back in the spring.

Wind rustling through the leaves drew my attention upward. The sky had transformed to a deeper, more solemn shade of blue. Puffy clouds glowed in soft shades of rose and peach, their edges tinged with gold in the dying light.

Powerful waves of love suddenly washed over me, through me, and around me with a force so intense that I had to hold onto my chair for a minute to steady myself. Pure, radiant love, with a strength and clarity I had not known in my earthly life surrounded and embraced me.

Face tilted to the heavens, I gratefully opened myself to receive this rich abundance of love so freely and joyfully given. I basked in the glow, bathed in it, until I was completely saturated, filled to the brim.

I knew at once where this energy was coming from. It could only be from David, sending me this heavenly love to reassure me that he was okay. More than okay. He had made it to the Other Side and his transition had been smooth—like stepping out into the unknown, taking a leap of faith and at the end of the journey, arriving home safely.

Could I say he was happy? I don't know. Happy is a funny word. It seems more like a word that belongs to this Earth, not an otherworldly one. Content? No, it was a much stronger feeling than contentment. Radiant? Definitely. Joyful? Yes, I believe so. It was hard to think about joy right at that moment, but I was certain that those waves of love flowing over me brought peace to my confused mind and serenity to my lonely soul.

Sometime later, I answered the door. Peter, my precious son, was standing on the front porch. He was worried about me and didn't want me to be alone that first awful night. I was happy to see him, to look at his beloved, familiar face.

He stared at me in surprise. "Mom ... you look fine!"

"Yes, I'm all right. I feel like I'm riding a wave of peace and love," I replied. "And I'll keep on riding it until I crash."

Under the covers in bed that night, those steady waves continued with a rhythm I found soothing. It felt as if David was wrapping me, swaddling me, cocooning me in his sacred arms to share his experience with me. Perhaps he was trying to shelter me from the ravages of panic and fear that would inevitably take over my life, as time swept him further away from me and I was left to walk into the unknown.

The feelings were stronger than any I'd ever known before in our earthly realm. I did not expect to feel that way. I'd been unable to think beyond the cruel reality that death brings. But on this night, I felt the richness of abundant love and the protection of a thousand singing angels. I felt treasured beyond anything I could ever imagine, and I slept better than I had in years.

*Wendy Willow*

# IDLE WAKE

When my parents moved to an old house on Mobile Bay in Alabama for their retirement, they needed to give their new homestead a name. They chose "Idle Wake," a nautical term for vessel speed that refers to slow, steady movement to prevent making waves—a suitable metaphor for retirement. After combing the beach for driftwood, I found a large, flat piece that would be suitable for a sign, then painted the new name. It hung with pride for decades on the garden shed next to their back porch.

My dad, Ralph Douglas, Sr. was a Search & Rescue pilot in the United States Coast Guard after graduating from Kesler Air Force Base in Biloxi, Mississippi and the Pensacola Navy Base in Florida. This was a mighty big step for a boy raised milking cows on his father's dairy farm in rural Alabama. He then flew hundreds of missions from Miami, Alaska, the Philippines, Newfoundland, and Thailand and received his wings for fixed-wing aircraft and helicopters in the early 1940s. His name is included among the Coast Guard's earliest pilots. He had earned a little idle wake time.

They spent many happy years on the bay entertaining family and teaching two grandsons about marine life and boating skills. Daddy continued to help people, occasionally rescuing boaters who became stranded on the bay after wind or mechanical failure. He even built parts and repaired boats from his home machine shop.

In 2000, my dad was diagnosed with terminal cancer. His illness gave us the opportunity to spend many days together watching the bay and having long discussions about his life and death. Mom would have nothing to do with these conversations or any talk of dying, including her own. My dad jokingly promised that he would "send us a sign" from the other side. Soon after he passed, Mom noticed lights flickering in the house and small items inexplicably moved from place to place, but she didn't believe in life after death, so she just laughed at the idea that these represented Daddy sending us signs.

In 2005, Hurricane Katrina sent a twelve-foot tidal surge up Mobile Bay that crashed into my parents' living room and flooded the house, leaving debris, mud, and crabs confused by their new surroundings. The Idle Wake sign washed away along with furniture and family photo albums from a lifetime of travel. I had never seen Mom so devastated and depressed as we shoveled flotsam and jetsam and memories from her home.

Mom loved the view of the sun rising over Mobile Bay from her living room and the memories that she and Daddy shared there in their retirement. She didn't want to live anyplace else. And so, we gradually rebuilt the house, piece by piece, recovering what we could find in the swamps that now surrounded the property.

A few years later, I took Mom out for a day of shopping and lunch. After a couple of hours of retail therapy, we decided it was time for a lunch break, but we were in a part of Mobile that was unfamiliar. Luckily, I had recently purchased a fundraiser booklet from the local high school that was filled with discount coupons. We found a coupon for a restaurant that seemed to be nearby; consulting our giant paper map we discovered the restaurant was only a few blocks away. It was one of those family-owned seafood places with lots of nautical memorabilia, like anchors, fish nets, and port holes on the walls for decoration. We were shown to a small table in the center of the crowded room, handed menus, and offered glasses of iced tea.

As I glanced up from my menu, I noticed a look of shock on Mom's face. "You look like you've seen a ghost," I said.

After a long pause, she carefully responded, "Look behind you."

I hesitantly turned in my chair and spotted our old Idle Wake sign hanging on the wall above my head. We were speechless! How did it get there? How long had it been there? Who put it there?

Our waitress said she knew nothing about it but agreed to ask the owner when he got back from running an errand. Finally, he appeared at our table, and we anxiously inquired how that sign—*our* sign—ended up in his restaurant.

The restaurant owner was oddly defensive at first, as Mom and I overwhelmed him with questions, but we gradually put all the puzzle pieces together. The owner explained that his brother had previously lived on Mobile Bay—right next door to my mom's house, as it turned out. When he was helping his brother to clean up after the hurricane, he found the sign and thought it would be perfect for his restaurant. It looked to him like ideal wall décor fitting the restaurant's nautical theme.

I now think the whole day was set-up from spirit, from the decision to go out with Mom, to being a little bit lost in Mobile, to the coupon book leading us to a restaurant where the sign was hanging the whole time. Daddy kept his promise and sent us an actual sign, our sign: the Idle Wake.

The day was a profound turning point in Mom's life that helped her to believe in life after death. Daddy did more than just send a sign that day; he showed us that he is closer than we think. Mom didn't join Daddy until 2019, but she lived the rest of her days with a quiet knowing that he was always with her and would show up when she least expected him.

*Maria Douglas Rosso*

# BEDTIME STORY SURPRISE

*A*s the mother of three boys, I often chuckle at the idea of a bedtime routine. Our routine can be an impromptu wrestling match or even an unexpected fort-building session. However, one thing that always captures my boys' attention: they love hearing stories from my childhood. A glimpse of what my life looked like at their age never fails to settle them into a state of attentive bedtime listening.

One school night a few years ago, when my kids were in elementary school, I used the "Do you want to hear a fun story from when I was your age?" strategy to get them settled into their beds. They got comfortable and I settled in the cozy reading chair. Then I began telling them about the day my late Grandpa Larry bought me a little black pony.

Not sure how many details my brain would retrieve that late in the day, I surprised myself. As I rocked back and forth in the big, upholstered chair, my soul journeyed back to my eight-year-old self, and the vivid details of the day I got my pony emerged effortlessly. Everything came back to me: the sounds, the colors, and the emotions.

I recounted how I bounced up and down in the front cab of my grandpa's truck because the road was so bumpy, and how excited I felt as we pulled into the parking lot of the sale barn. I described the white wooden bleacher seats that encircled the dusty dirt arena.

The auctioneer had talked so loud and fast as he identified the bids that the people in the stands called out for the cows, pigs, horses, and sheep as they paraded around the arena. I tried to duplicate his voice for my sleepy boys.

Most importantly, I was flooded with the feeling I remembered from when the little black pony entered the arena and my eyes and face lit up. Details kept unfolding as if I were sitting right next to my grandfather on those white, dust-covered bleachers.

"Did you know you were going to get a pony?" my sons asked.

"No, I think Grandpa Larry just decided to buy it when he saw how excited I was as the little pony trotted into the arena."

He had started bidding immediately, and my heart was thrumming with excitement as our bid of $100 won!

"Did you get to keep the pony?" the boys wanted to know.

"I did!" I recalled the joy I felt when my new pony stepped off the trailer onto my grandparents' farm. I have countless memories of riding my pony while visiting my grandparents' farm. "Grandpa Larry gave me a gift I will never forget."

I could sense the boys glowing with the same happiness I had felt that day with my grandpa. After some brief bedtime prayers, I kissed them goodnight. Then I headed down the hallway toward my bedroom.

As I stepped into my room, I was halted in my tracks by a potent whiff of my grandpa's Old Spice cologne. The smell was so strong that I leaned back, as if to keep the spray from getting in my eyes! It had been twenty years since I smelled that cologne, but the scent was so recognizably my grandpa's that I immediately knew he was present.

Surprised and shocked by the encounter, I rushed into the bathroom to tell my husband what had just happened. In a split second, it all made sense to me. My grandpa had been listening as I recounted the details of the day he bought me a pony. It was his help that made the story flow flawlessly. He was sharing in the love and joy of my memory. With a puff of his cologne, he let me know he had been our bedtime story guest.

*Audrey Burns*

# THE EXTRA A1 TILE

The plastic grocery bags bite into my wrists along with the purse straps and laptop bag dangling from my arms. It's dark, yet I know the path well. I kick off my shoes without reaching for the light and trudge up the stairs. My weary mind races through a litany of questions, not wanting to acknowledge that the answers reflect a life totally out of balance.

*When was the last time I ate? What can I make to eat quickly so I can get to bed? How long have I been up today?* What does it matter? I don't sleep anyway.

*Ow!* Instinctively shifting my weight to avoid the pain from the object under my foot, I wonder—*What have I just stepped on?*

Unceremoniously relieving my tired arms by dumping their burden on the kitchen counter, I move in the direction of the light switch across the kitchen to avoid the item on the floor. Flicking on the light, I turn to investigate what has interrupted my path.

A Scrabble tile with the letter A and the number 1, indicating the point value, stares back at me.

*How can this be?* It has been months since anyone has played Scrabble in this house. I swept the floor this morning as the coffee was brewing. This object was not there.

*No one has been in the house for the past nineteen hours.*

As I mentally catalog these facts, I keep staring at the tile. It sits directly in the center of the entry to the kitchen. *There is no way I missed seeing this when I swept the floor. No way I could have avoided stepping on it as I gathered my things to leave, so many hours ago.*

Crumbling to the floor, I scoop up the tile and begin to sob uncontrollably. "Thank you! Thank you! Thank you!"

Memories flood the screen of my mind like a movie's highlights reel. Sitting at the kitchen table playing Scrabble with my oldest son. The sound of his laughter as he played a high scoring word. The generous smile on his face as he promised, "You'll win next time, Mom." Hugging each other as we completed a game, the winner graciously putting the game away.

*If only I could hug him one more time.*

The tears flow freely now as I remember our time together playing this board game. I recall the healthy competition of who scored the most points with one word or who laid down the longest word in each game. I can hear his siblings impatiently inquiring if we are ever going to finish. Our games stretched on for a long time because we allowed one another to think extensively, to craft the word with the most points. I understand now, and I think we both instinctively knew, the time spent together was the most important thing—not completing the game.

The A1 represents my oldest son, Aaron. He is letting me know I am not alone. He sees me, now, when no one else seems to. He acknowledges my broken heart and that I am doing the best I can. His message tells me I am loved. He is here with me.

*Thank you! I need this!* I have been overwhelmed dealing with my grief at his passing and his sister's extended hospitalization.

As my weariness evaporates, the logical portion of my engineering brain wants to know *how* this tile appeared. It searches for a rational explanation. *It must have been under the refrigerator or stove and the broom ferreted it out as I swept this morning.*

Frantically digging out the box with the Scrabble game from the storage area, I am determined to get to the bottom of the mystery. Carrying the box upstairs to desk, I fire up the computer and search for how many tiles, by letter, are included in a game. I meticulously lay out the tiles in the box to match the lines on the computer screen. The mystery tile still lays on the kitchen counter to ensure it does not get erroneously mixed in.

As the last wooden tile from the game is categorized, I realize the pieces in the box represent a complete set. There is no missing A1.

My oldest son's death by suicide at the age of sixteen swept the rest of our family of five into a tornado of emotional devastation. As our family tried to navigate the extreme emotional fluctuations in Aaron's mental health prior to his death, without any real answers of why things were happening, my first marriage of almost seventeen years dissolved.

My daughter, our youngest, has struggled outwardly and I've been performing an extreme intervention to prevent the possibility of her following in her brother's footsteps. My days consist of juggling a new full-time job, trying to make financial ends meet as a single person, and traveling ninety minutes each way, seven days a week, to the hospital to see my daughter and meet with her medical team.

And now, in the middle of this emotional chaos, I have arrived home to find the Scrabble tile. The message of being loved, acknowledged, and validated that I am not alone is inherently clear to me. This tiny wooden square represents a life raft for my emotional state. I know I will keep the

A1 tile as a memento forever and a precious reminder that support is always there, if only we will pause to ask and receive.

*Roxanne Hupp*

# PURRS FROM THE BEYOND

*Y*ears ago, I had a grey tabby cat that was my absolute favorite being in the world. He was a soul-mate cat, indeed. His name was Thomas, a name that will forever hold a special place in my heart. Thomas wasn't just a pet; he was a dear companion who had an uncanny way of understanding and comforting me.

I'd often find him gazing at me with a curious and joyful look in his eyes. He observed me as though he were captivated by some unseen wonder. The pure joy and radiant love in his gaze was as if he were experiencing constant revelations. In these moments, I felt an inexplicable connection with him. He seemed to hold the key to hidden knowledge.

He was nineteen years old when his health began to decline. Our bond grew even stronger in his final months. We'd share quiet moments and his purring was a soothing melody that calmed my soul. His presence was a comfort, a reminder that love is a powerful force that knows no bounds.

But as the seasons changed, Thomas's health began to falter more quickly. The night before he passed, in a moment of sorrow, I had looked into his eyes and made a heartfelt request. It wasn't whispered; it was spoken out loud, a plea to my best fur-friend.

"Thomas," I said, through my tears, "if it's possible, give me a sign from the other side. Send me another cat, even if it's just a single encounter. And please let it be a cat that bears your resemblance."

As I made my request, Thomas responded with a soft, comforting purr, as though he was reassuring me that he understood and would do his best to grant my request.

At last, I came to the heart-wrenching realization that the time had come to say our goodbyes, to let him go in peace. Holding him in my arms, I whispered my final words of love and gratitude into his ears as he took his last breath. In that poignant instant, I felt his spirit slip away, leaving a void in my heart.

However, our connection transcended the boundaries of life and death.

Exactly three days after Thomas's passing, I was walking out onto my back patio when, out of nowhere, a loudly purring cat raced right through the open door and into my house! It was as if he was being chased, moving with urgency and determination. This cat, which I later found out was named Jack, was the spitting image of Thomas.

The soft grey and black fur, the curious eyes, and the pure joy in his gaze was apparent. Although Jack was quite a bit younger than Thomas had been, the similarity in their appearance was striking. There was no doubt in my mind that Thomas had orchestrated this encounter from the beyond, just as I had requested.

I stood there in shock as Jack quickly explored every room in our house. He was on some sort of mission. It was clear that he had a purpose, a message to deliver.

Overwhelmed by my emotions, I ended up sitting on the kitchen floor, coaxing the cat to approach. I embraced him warmly, a gesture he wholeheartedly welcomed. As he purred contently, I knew that this was the sign I had asked for. It was such a powerful moment, creating a connection that helped to heal me.

Jack continued to visit from time to time during the next four years. As it turns out, Jack was a legendary figure in our part of town. He was known as "the neighborhood cat," even though he had owners. Jack had a knack for liberating food from people's porches and redistributing it to the stray cats, a charming idiosyncrasy that endeared him to many.

Eventually, we got word that Jack needed a new home. With no hesitation, my spouse and I gratefully opened our hearts and home to him, and he seamlessly became part of our lives, full-time.

Thirteen years have passed. We still have Jack. He's the same age now as Thomas was before he left the physical. Now more than ever, he bears a striking resemblance to our beloved Thomas. His soft gray fur and wise, joyful eyes are a constant reminder of the connection that transcends the boundaries of life and death.

Like Thomas, Jack's body is starting to grow old. Yet when I think of Jack crossing over the rainbow bridge, I take comfort in knowing that he, like Thomas, will still be with us in spirit. And what is a "bridge" anyway? It is a pathway to another destination, a connection that is left wide open.

*Shannon Shade*

# GOING FOR GOLD NUGGETS

he couple in the front row did not radiate the same open energy as the others in my workshop. They sat solemnly, only semi-engaged in what I was sharing. As my gaze passed over them, I paused, snagged by a wispy image that appeared both in the room with us and on the screen of my mind.

There, between the man and woman, stood a young boy who clearly belonged to them. The vision lasted only a moment, but long enough for me to see him give me a friendly wave.

I'd been teaching for almost two hours, so I called for a break. The man headed immediately for the restrooms and the woman moved toward the exit. Now on a mission, I followed her outside. Being early in the first part of the workshop, I hadn't yet spoken to many participants, so I greeted her and learned her name is Robin Brown

I said, "I don't usually sense spirits when I'm not doing private readings, but I just saw a young boy who I feel is your son standing between you and your husband."

I could tell by her wide eyes and the brief nod of her head that Robin did, indeed, have a son across the veil.

She seemed at a loss for words, so I said, "I didn't sense a message other than his desire to let you know he's here with you. And I know he's fine because he very clearly waved at me."

Robin thanked me and I returned to the front of the room to review my syllabus. A few minutes later, just as I was about to start up the class, she stepped beside me.

"I hope you don't mind, but my husband, Scott, is going to sit out this next part of the workshop. After I told him what you said, he needs some time to get himself together."

I felt a sudden fear that my message had upset them, but what Robin shared next removed any worry.

She explained that their teenage son, Doug, had recently passed from cancer. Every day since their son's transition, Scott would go into Doug's room and sit on his bed. He would face the wall where a photo of Doug's hand was tacked to a bulletin board. He used the cut-out hand as a focal point while he chatted with his son, sharing the day's events and any thoughts he wanted him to know.

Robin told me that she and Scott had traveled from Wisconsin to learn in my workshop how to better connect with Doug. She shook her head in wonder as she reported, "Scott just told me that he had a special chat with Doug in his bedroom before we left on this trip. It turns out he looked at the hand on the bulletin board and said, 'Doug, I don't know how this spirit communication works, but if there's any way you can let us know you're still with us, maybe you can wave at us.'"

Robin and I looked in each other's eyes and shared a moment of silent celebration. At that point in my mediumship journey, I could count on the fingers of one hand the number of times a spirit person had revealed themself to me outside of a reading. Doug had done so by directly responding to his father's specific request.

I rejoiced in the awareness that now Robin and Scott would know their son existed beyond his physical body. To solidify this knowing, I wanted to offer them the gift of a private session.

They eagerly accepted my offer of a phone reading. It didn't matter that we couldn't meet in person. I knew that, from his state of consciousness beyond space and time, Doug would be able to join the three of us.

When Thanksgiving came, the day had a special feel to it. I imagined the joy the Brown family would feel when they realized that Doug would be enjoying the holiday with them.

I greeted Robin and Scott on the phone at the appointed time and I felt Doug's presence immediately.

"Doug just said the word *ranger*," I reported.

Robin gasped and I knew I had struck a chord. Buoyed by her reaction, I listened even more intently.

"Now he says, "Ranger *Rick*."

Hearing this, Robin began crying. "Did he really just say that?" she asked between jagged breaths.

"That's very significant," Scott added.

There are moments in most readings when those in spirit give the kind of evidence that I call "gold nuggets." As I would learn later, this qualified as a validation so significant that we could have ended the session then and there and Doug's parents would have known we were enjoying a two-way connection with their son.

I spent the rest of the session, however, describing Doug's unique personality traits, memories, and most importantly, the messages he wanted to share with his family.

When the reading concluded, Robin shared with me why she had been so shocked with what came through. She explained that Doug loved to visit his grandfather's farm. He was too young to get a driver's license, but one of his favorite pastimes while there was to drive his grandfather's farm vehicles.

His favorite was a utility four-wheeler with the model name "Ranger" emblazoned on the side. Every vehicle on the farm had a name, and this one was affectionately known as Ranger Rick.

I experienced a rush of gratitude when I sent the Browns a digital recording of the reading by email. There in my inbox was a photo of Robin, Scott, and Doug—riding Ranger Rick. Their broad smiles showed me why Doug had chosen this memory to validate his presence.

Hours later, I received an unexpected email from Robin's father regarding the reading. I smiled to realize that Robin had wasted no time sharing the recording with other family members. Doug's grandfather admitted in his email that he had been wary of his daughter sitting with a medium. He explained that he didn't want anyone to cause her more pain than his grandson's passing had already brought upon the family.

"I'm a retired Marine Corps lieutenant colonel," he wrote, as if to show me that he was not easily duped. "When I listened to that recording, I tried to pick it apart, but there is no way you could have known about Ranger Rick. I tried to think what I might share if I were on the other side to let people know it was me, and that was it."

My smile turned to laughter when I read the colonel's final words. Doug's grandfather, who had reached the equivalent rank in the Marines as I had in the Navy, ended his email by writing, "You done good, kid."

What I call "the after party" continued throughout the next day. Robin and Scott emailed me with additional validations as more family members listened to the reading. Most added to the true feeling of thanksgiving except for one. I learned from Scott that the session left Doug's sister feeling disappointed. Unbeknownst to anyone, she had hoped Doug would mention a special gift he had given her.

As I read this, I felt unexpectedly lightheaded. Attuning to the cause, I sensed a drop-in from the spirit of young Doug Brown. I clicked the "reply" button on Scott's email and excitedly pecked out the words, "Doug is here with me now!"

I love unexpected visits from those in spirit who I've met before. They are easily recognizable by their personality and the familiar images they put in my mind from past visits. This time, however, Doug showed me a vision I hadn't yet seen.

I quickly typed a description of what I was experiencing: "He's putting images in my head. He's showing me a ballerina. She's wearing a tutu. This has something to do with his sister. And now he's showing me a gorilla. I know you will understand why he has to get this through to you."

And with that, Doug stepped away.

"Let me know why this is so important to him," I finished, and hit "send" on the email to Scott.

Later that evening, I received a response with a photo attached. In the text of the email, Scott explained that Doug must have known that his sister was disappointed in the reading.

"Attached is an image from the website where Doug chose the special gift his sister wanted him to mention. When you see it, you'll understand why we're all so excited."

I clicked the attachment. When the image opened, I couldn't help but gasp just as Robin had when Doug shared the "Ranger Rick" gold nugget.

On the screen before me sat one ridiculously cute, very pink gorilla. I was correct that Doug's drop-in had something to do with his sister. But she wasn't the ballerina. It was the pink gorilla, dressed unmistakably in a ruffled tutu.

I pumped a fist in celebration of yet another "no other explanation" moment that would surely bring the Brown family the comfort and healing that are the goals of mediumship. They now knew beyond a doubt what I had discerned from the moment Doug waved at me in my workshop: Cancer may have taken his body, but his vibrant spirit was still very much a part of the family.

Scott's final words in our email exchange confirmed that they had received this message loud and clear, for he wrote back, "We are celebrating, Suzanne, because you just can't make up a gorilla in a tutu!"

*Suzanne Giesemann*

# PART THREE

*Deepening Your Connection
with the Divine*

*Only when you drink from the river of silence shall you indeed sing.*

— KHALIL GIBRAN

# THE CRITICAL KEYS OF ATTUNEMENT

ecause you are a soul, you are already equipped with what it takes to work as a medium and connect with loved ones and higher beings in the non-physical realms. Whether or not it's your calling to do so for others depends on what your soul chose to do in this lifetime.

Not to worry! This section is intended for anyone with an interest in spirit communication. Whether you are a professional medium, you want to connect with your loved ones in spirit, or you're simply curious as to how non-physical interactions take place, I will address you in the same way I would any student of mediumship.

As you may recall from Part 1, I am not what some call a "born medium." I uncovered my abilities through trial and error and sitting regularly in meditation with my guides. When I agreed to teach my first class in mediumship after years of doing readings as a professional, I took a close look at what works and what doesn't work when it comes to sensing and interacting with those across the veil.

My guides gave me the syllabus, but the absolute best teacher is personal experience. To this day, I use every experience of spirit connection to hone my skills. I recommend you do the same. After each meditation, after every time you sit to commune with a spirit, after any experience of sensing the presence of some spirit in your field of awareness—take note. Literally.

I have taught thousands of people to connect with higher consciousness using a seven-step process which I call The BLESS ME Method®. The instructions for this practice, which are covered in my book *The Awakened Way*, provide a specific routine one can follow to flow from normal waking consciousness to the optimal state for communicating with those in the spirit world.

While this method has proven valuable even for those who have been meditating for decades, the foundations that lie beneath the steps are what give it universal value. I have identified seven foundational elements that make for the best possible connection with any level of higher consciousness.

Here they are in brief:

- A Strong Belief in Spirit
- A Crystal-Clear Intention
- An Expanded State of Awareness
- A Shift in Self-Identification
- An Invitation and Willingness to Blend Fields
- A Deep and Abiding Trust in Spirit
- A Cooperative State of Flow

These foundational elements work together in mediumship. Used individually and collectively, they help you to bypass the brain's filters, get past your personal belief system, and overcome the body's dense energy, which are the main elements that block any human from sensing the spirit world.

Happily, none of these steps are particularly challenging. They do require, however, an understanding of why they are important and a commitment to putting them into practice. In so doing, you create new neural pathways and expand your energy field, thus using body and mind in new ways to take you from "only human" to soul-to-soul (spirit) communicator.

Let's now dive into each of these seven keys, to flesh out their deeper significance and how to use them in mediumship.

# A STRONG BELIEF IN SPIRIT

The first key to connecting with loved ones across the veil is *belief*. Communication with those in the spirit world is far more likely to occur if you genuinely believe that the spirit world is real and that you can communicate with those who inhabit it. If you doubt either of these things, your subconscious mind will create a very real vibrational block.

Henry Ford showed that he understood this principle quite well when he said, "Whether you believe you can do a thing or not, you are right."

Any lack of belief you may have in the spirit world or in your innate ability to connect across the veil can energetically close the door to those in spirit. Therefore, begin by examining your level of skepticism. It's wise to be skeptical when people describe paranormal phenomena, but it's equally wise to maintain an open mind. There is a big difference between being close-minded and being willing to "trust but verify," a quote attributed to Ronald Reagan!

Approaching mediumship with a sense of openness and anticipation allows you to play and experiment. With a childlike sense of wonder, welcome any adventures in consciousness, so long as they don't feel in any way harmful. If something you learn or experience doesn't sit right or clashes too much with your current belief system, that's okay. Set it aside, and if you're meant to give it further attention, it will come into your awareness again at a later time.

Before I became aware of the greater reality, I didn't believe in spirit guides and angels. I had no personal experience of the higher realms. Happily, my desire to connect with my stepdaughter across the veil led me to consider all possibilities. This attitude helped open a door to even greater realms of which I was entirely unaware. Guides and angels subsequently used that opening to make their presence known to me in such wondrous ways that I could not deny their existence and I let down my human defenses.

Today, I welcome all benevolent experiences that will help my soul's evolution and serve the greater good, including those that might at first seem silly or outlandish. I recommend you do the same.

## A CRYSTAL-CLEAR INTENTION

Thoughts and desires are the tools with which we dip into the sea of all possibilities and manifest an outcome. While in human form, we may be limited in how much control we have over any one outcome. Our desired results are far more likely to occur, however, when we couple our actions with clear, focused intention.

Applying this principle to mediumship, feel the difference in the following two examples of intentions:

- I would really like to connect with a spirit across the veil.
- I intend to establish an unmistakable connection with any spirit being who can help serve the greatest and highest good for me and all concerned.

The first sentence is a lukewarm desire. It feels a bit needy with a tiny dose of doubt hanging over it. Grieving people can grow frustrated in their attempts to sense their loved ones across the veil, trying harder and harder to connect. Rather than holding a trust-filled intention, they send out what is more akin to a plea.

Energy flows where consciousness goes. Harness the creative power of consciousness to turn your desires into actuality. The second sentence is a strong affirmation that carries the energy of a fait accompli. It radiates purpose and a powerful motive of service to self and others.

Don't simply sit and hope to connect. Visualize your desired outcome before you establish any mediumship connection. Know exactly what you hope to accomplish and find the most powerful words possible to give that goal wings.

Intention focuses free will and transmutes desire into a force that manifests. Couple belief with intention, and you have harnessed two key ingredients in our recipe for making a connection with the higher realms.

## AN EXPANDED STATE OF AWARENESS

When we are caught up in the human story, it is easy to become blinded to the deeper levels of reality. The physical senses continuously pull our awareness in different directions. Our minds are bombarded with information coming at us at ever increasing speeds. Social media and smart phones have turned attention deficit from a disorder into the new order of things.

It's no wonder most people overlook the still, small voice within. They can't hear it through all the mental noise.

Higher beings are all around us. To attune to the higher frequencies, we must not only raise our frequency, but cut down on the static. The tried-and-true way to do this is to sit in silence and focus on one thing to the exclusion of other distractions. You might have heard of this practice. It's called meditation!

When my stepdaughter passed, I had an epiphany when I saw her lifeless body. I knew immediately that it wasn't Susan in the coffin. And I somehow knew that the vibrant energy of Susan couldn't have simply disappeared.

I made it my mission to connect with her spirit, even though I had not given real credence to the existence of a non-physical part of us until that moment. I knew that there were people called mediums who could allegedly communicate with deceased loved ones, but I wanted to sense Susan myself.

I began meditating that very week. This was in 2006 when meditation wasn't as mainstream as it is today. I was living on my sailboat at the time and didn't have access to the internet or books on meditation. Instead, I sat dutifully each day, closed my eyes, and asked Susan to make her presence known to me.

I sat quietly for about twenty minutes a day, concentrating on that singular, all-important goal of sensing Susan. I quickly noticed that my own thoughts kept popping up ... useless, trivial, distracting, annoying thoughts and irrelevant images. I simply set aside anything that didn't feel like it came from Susan. In the beginning, that was everything. And then, I went back to waiting for Susan to make her presence known.

Little did I know that I had stumbled upon an outstanding method to train my mind for mediumship. I was slowing down the busy mind and experiencing the coherent, whole brain states that are optimal for practicing mediumship.

Neuroscientists have measured and identified the frequency patterns of the brain while it is engaged in various activities. These brainwaves are the result of electrical activity produced by neurons, the specialized nerves of the brain. The five brainwave states described below are associated with specific states of consciousness.

In beta state, the brain emits brainwaves between fourteen and thirty hertz, or cycles per second. This is the state of normal waking consciousness. If we were to attach an electroencephalogram (EEG) device to your skull now as you read these words, your brain would be emitting waves within the beta range.

With one or more deep, slow, intention-filled breaths, the frequency of your brainwaves would slow down. When they fall within the range of nine to thirteen hertz, you would be in the alpha brainwave state. This expanded state of awareness in which the body is relaxed but the mind is still alert is ideal for sensing the presence of spirits and communicating with them.

If you allow yourself to sink into deeper states of awareness, your brainwaves will slow even more. Theta brainwave frequencies measure between four and eight hertz. This highly relaxed, semi-conscious to unconscious state lends itself to experiences of directly channeling those across the veil. The deeper the state of consciousness, the less the medium will filter the communications from those sharing messages.

Beyond theta lies the state of deep, dreamless sleep known as delta. In this non-aware condition, the brain measures less than four brainwave cycles per second.

Scientists are now aware of a range of brain frequencies higher than beta. Patterns that exceed thirty hertz are called gamma waves and involve a heightened sense of perception. High performing athletes and experienced meditators have been shown to exhibit a higher abundance of gamma waves. These brain states can lead to deep spiritual experiences resulting from the sharp concentration and focus that gamma waves allow.

It is not necessary to know exactly the frequency of waves your brain is emitting when you sit to connect with spirit. The key is to remain aware that normal waking consciousness—your beta brainwave state—is not conducive to spirit communication.

Due to my single-minded goal of connecting with my stepdaughter, I honed the ability to focus intently and to intentionally drop into the ideal brainwave states for mediumship. I did not achieve this goal overnight.

In fact, it took me several years until I had my first sacred visit from Susan. Much later, she told me that she had deliberately held back from making her presence known because I had so many other skills to learn in the meantime. She was right. The more I sat in the silence, holding onto the unwavering intention of connecting with Susan, the more I learned how it feels to be in the non-ordinary states of awareness.

In the early days of my practice, I studied the work of Robert Monroe, who pioneered the use of binaural beats to achieve a coherent, whole-brain state. I used a variety of recordings that were infused with frequencies that lead the brain to various states of consciousness.

I learned how it feels to be in the expanded state that results from alpha waves vs. the deeper meditative experiences of the theta brainwave state. This self-led training allowed me to be able to drop into alpha or theta at will, a valuable skill for mediumship.

Does this kind of training really work? Absolutely. Several respected research scientists in different laboratories in the United States have put my mediumship to the test. During one such session, the researcher fitted me with an electroencephalogram (EEG) device. As he was hooking up the nest of wires in a cap on my skull, I decided to access the familiar alpha state I enter for doing readings, even before being instructed to do so. I self-induced the slower brainwaves simply by taking a few slow, deep breaths and setting the intention to drop into alpha. As I did so, the scientist turned to me and asked with surprise, "Are you an experienced meditator?"

I didn't know how to answer him. In terms of years of practice, I knew that there were many people who had been meditating decades longer than I had. For that reason, I shrugged and replied, "I suppose I am. Why do you ask?"

He shook his head as he stared at his computer screen and replied, "We haven't even started our experiments yet, and you're already producing some very coherent alpha waves."

As one who strives to obtain evidence, I appreciated his comment. It provided validation that training my mind and body to become coherent had worked. If your goal is to be the best medium possible, to serve to the utmost of your ability as the voice for those who longer have a physical voice, then you will commit yourself to sitting in the silence regularly, if not daily, and expanding your state of awareness.

Many types of meditation suggest focusing on the breath. This leads to an enjoyable state of relaxation and will most definitely help to slow down a busy mind—but for some people, it can also lead to the restlessness and wandering mind they are hoping to overcome. I have learned that simply paying attention to the breath is not enough for mediumship practice. Focusing on direct contact with higher beings—perhaps even one specific being—coupled with a relaxed body and alert mind are the keys to connecting.

I suggest this sequence to begin each meditative session or mediumship reading: First, remind yourself of your intention. Notice your level of tension or stress and give it a rating from one to ten before you take your first intentional breath. Then take as many slow, deep breaths as it takes to shift from normal, waking consciousness to expanded awareness. Inhale slowly to the count of four or five and exhale to the count of six or seven.

As you do so, use autosuggestions to relax as much as possible, gently telling your mind to be calm. After several breaths, rate your tension level again. Ideally, it will have decreased.

Be aware that an alert mind is quite different from a busy mind. Your goal is to remain alert yet create space between your normal thoughts, so that when those in spirit reach out, you notice their presence.

As a further benefit of regularly expanding your consciousness, you might find you experience more peace throughout your day. Your intuition will grow stronger. Both positive effects will directly benefit your mediumship.

Be aware that you may not experience spiritually transformative experiences or sense the presence of individual spirits each time you sit in the silence. There may be days when you feel that nothing has happened at all. Remember that meditation is the training ground for mediumship. In the meantime, trust that Spirit knows what you need in every moment and enjoy the journey.

# A SHIFT IN SELF-IDENTIFICATION

Remember that the reason you can communicate with non-physical souls is because you are also a soul. Most humans remain unaware of our dual nature as souls having a physical experience. The brain's programming keeps us focused on our physical senses and the objective world, often to the exclusion of our inner world, where we perceive most mediumistic connections.

During my in-person classes, I like to demonstrate how the spirit world is right here and accessible through a simple shift in awareness. I hand out a paper covered with the repeating image of red roses. I instruct the participants to hold the paper to their nose and slowly move it away while gazing softly with unfocused eyes at the center of the page. When the page gets about eighteen inches from the nose, a murmur of surprise and delight passes through the room.

Their actions have revealed a three-dimensional heart of roses that appears to be floating in front of the page!

I invite them to notice that a simple shift in focus has revealed a 3-D object that was hidden in plain sight within a two-dimensional page. I also emphasize that even though the 3-D heart appears separate from the page, it is an integral part of the underlying "reality."

The heart of roses trick is clearly an optical illusion. I use it strictly as an analogy for what happens when we shift our focus from our three-dimensional world and reveal the higher dimensions of Spirit. This all-important shift is not done with the eyes. It is a dimensional shift that occurs within the mind.

Another analogy that proves helpful when understanding the shift that makes spirit communication possible is that of a TV remote control. Imagine you want to watch a movie on your television. This intention initiates a series of actions. You decide what movie you want to watch, and you determine what channel it's on. You pick up the remote control and turn on the TV.

Next, you press a button for the desired channel. You don't concern yourself with how the remote control works and if the right channel will show up. You trust that in pushing the button, the movie will begin playing on the screen. And remember, just as you know that the signals are available to your TV any time you choose to turn it on, those in spirit are ever available as it serves the greater good.

In mediumship, the mind is your remote control. You hold the intention of connecting with one spirit or a group of beings with whom you wish to communicate. You may also decide to simply let the mind "surf" the spirit world for an interaction that will be helpful and healing.

In any case, to metaphorically "push the button" and bring up the desired experience, state the word "Shift!" either silently or aloud. Your intention and the act of stating the word opens you to the desired experience.

As you make this shift, hold in awareness what it is you are shifting *to* as well as what you are shifting *from*. You are shifting from limited human awareness to your more expanded state as the soul that you are. You are temporarily setting aside your identification of being "The Story of You" and opening to the awareness that you are so much more than your temporary human tale.

Why do we have to make this shift so deliberately? It is because we need to overcome the brain's programming. Its filters keep you from being aware of your dual nature as both human and soul at the same time. To understand this, think of a drawing you may have seen of two black vases positioned so that a shift in perspective causes you to see the white space in between them as a face.

For the briefest of moments, by holding a strong intention, you can see both the two vases and the face at the same time. Quickly, however, the brain focuses your attention on either the vases or the face. It takes conscious effort to shift back and forth. You do this by making an intentional choice as to which image you want to see from within the wholeness of the drawing.

It is the same with the medium's shift. You are both a soul and a human at the same time, but it takes conscious effort to learn to shift back and forth.

Einstein said that no problem can be solved from the level at which it originated. He knew that as whole, multidimensional beings, we can access more than one level. The choice to make a conscious shift instantly allows you access to a higher perspective that is always available and the insights that flow from the higher levels.

The shift to the higher dimensions is a subtle movement in awareness, but it is quite powerful. In fact, in the Spiritualist tradition, this shift is called "stepping into the Power," because it allows us to access the life force that unites all of creation. It is the ultimate wholeness. Since you cannot technically be *out* of the Power, "stepping into the Power" takes what we know at a subconscious level—that we are more than just human—and brings this awareness to your conscious mind.

This deliberate shift also notifies those in the spirit world that you are here for them and are ready to connect.

All of these preparatory keys are very much akin to the process you go through when you want to connect two wireless devices, such as pairing a smartphone with a portable speaker. The first thing you do is make both devices "discoverable." It is your strong belief, clear intention, and expanded state of awareness that make you discoverable to the spirit world.

Now you are "ready to pair." The shift takes you to that blinking light state where you are searching for the other with which you will pair. The next two foundational steps ensure that you will end up connected.

# AN INVITATION TO BLEND FIELDS

Those in the spirit world become aware of your efforts to communicate with them from the moment the desire arises within you. As you are readying yourself by expanding your consciousness and shifting your focus to the spirit world, they are adjusting their frequency as well.

A medium, as the word implies, is an intermediary between the physical and non-physical dimensions. You mentally "meet the spirits in the middle." You can either sit quietly and notice who may be present in your field, or you can ramp up the power by issuing a loving invitation to those in spirit to come into your awareness. Examples of appropriate invitations include, "Come now," "Step close," or even, "Let's dance!"

The more heartfelt this invitation, the easier the connection. To raise your vibration, simply generate the innate qualities of your soul such as love, kindness, compassion, and gratitude as you welcome spirits into your field of awareness. The higher vibrations that you radiate as you do so make it much easier for those in spirit to merge and blend with you.

We call other realities the higher realms for a reason. Our physical world is quite dense compared to the spirit realms. Those in the spirit world must lower their vibration to communicate with us. Spirit communication is much more likely to occur when we raise our frequency to meet those in spirit.

This explains why desperation is counterproductive when connecting across the veil. Trying hard, worrying, complaining, and/or experiencing the fear and longing that accompany a dire need to connect reflects a lack of trust in the process and in Spirit. Such energies constrict our field rather than expand it.

The spiritual laws of Complementarity and Reciprocation assure us of balance in all things. These laws state, "What you give out, you get back." In other words, if you want to establish a connection with those in the higher realms, you must give them your own higher energy.

Of course, if you are grieving, it is hard to lift your spirits to meet those on the other side. When grief is especially heavy, it is helpful to ask specifically for the sorrow to be set aside as you are setting the intention to connect. When you are not trying to connect, be sure to allow yourself to feel the pain. This is a necessary part of the healing process.

As you invite spirits to blend their fields with yours, pause and gauge your energy. Picture a spirit gazing upon your aura and imagine what they would see. Would your energy field be bright and sparkly or dull and constricted? Your aura is dynamic, changing moment by moment depending upon the thoughts and emotions with which you empower it.

An excellent technique to ensure that you are giving as good as you get is to think of a traffic light with its red, yellow, and green lenses. For this analogy, the color isn't what matters. The meaning we give to each light on the pole is the important point here. Humans around the world have agreed that red means stop, yellow means caution, and green means go.

When connecting with spirit, an energetic red light to the spirit world would be reflected by thoughts such as, "I'm not really sure the astral realm is real, so I don't know why I'm even trying. I probably won't have any luck."

A person with the following thoughts would be analogous to giving a yellow light to those in spirit. "I want to do this, but what if I fail? I guess I'm willing to try, though, so here goes."

Green light energy would arise from thoughts such as, "Spirit world, I am here for you! I am harnessing all my belief and faith and sending it to you with as much love and gratitude as humanly possible!"

A sensitive person can feel the clear energetic difference in these three phrases. Believe me, those in spirit can, too.

In an actual traffic signal, the same white light shines through each lens. The color of the lens determines how that light is perceived. The one light of Spirit shines through you at all times, as well as in the souls with whom you wish to communicate. To enjoy the clearest possible connection, turn up your heart light as you invite spirits to blend with you and project your communications through the lens of love.

# A DEEP AND ABIDING TRUST IN SPIRIT

When I connect with those in the spirit world, I usually don't see the way they looked when they were in the physical world. Instead, I see charades of meaningful motions. I see clear images of places and objects that they share with me. I may see specific features that serve as evidence, such as a large nose or a hand gnarled by arthritis, but I wouldn't be able to describe their overall appearance.

I don't know if this ability will ever develop, but I have finally embraced this facial "blindness" for the gift that it is. Not being able to see the spirits has forced me to trust that they are present when I invite them to merge with me. It has led me to trust that they will show me, in a multitude of clever ways, who they are and what messages they want to share.

This confidence has come from doing readings with the awareness that Spirit will never let me down. One healing reading after another has proven to me that the spirit world is real and that we can trust that higher beings will do whatever is needed to make their presence known. I have learned that the only one who can let me down is me, and then only by not believing and not offering my full faith and love to those in spirit.

Trust that the same is true for you and all souls.

When you invite a spirit to communicate with you and your motive is for comfort, healing, and growth for all concerned, trust that just the right spirit will show up, even if it's not the person you expected or hoped to hear from. If you tune in and sense no one, do not place blame on anyone. Trust that there is a reason for what may seem to be a failure. Ask for guidance and learn from every interaction.

Spirit always wants whatever is the highest and best outcome for all involved. From our limited human perspective, we may not always know what that is. Therefore, train yourself to set all assumptions and expectations aside about how a spirit connection will unfold. Be willing to admit that you don't have all the answers and that you never work alone.

## A COOPERATIVE STATE OF FLOW

When you enjoy a pleasant, casual conversation with someone, you might later talk about the experience by saying, "It just flowed." This is how to envision spirit communication as well.

Enter each spirit conversation with a sense of wonder and an anything is possible mindset, as in, "I wonder how this reading or meditation is going to unfold? I can't wait to see!" And then, just as you do in a normal human conversation, simply relax and set all effort aside.

Do this now as an exercise:

Visualize yourself talking with someone in person. How much effort do you exert? Tune in to what your body is experiencing as you create an imaginary exchange in your mind. You say something, and the other person responds. You don't know where the conversation may go, so you flow with what arises as the other puts their two cents in.

Now, imagine you can't hear well. What do you do to attune better? You focus more intently on what they're saying, noticing verbal cues to fill in the blanks of any missed words. You may lean in closer. You may ask the other person to speak up. Because there's not much more you can do to improve communications, you simply relax and interact. It's natural. And so is mediumship.

Many humans think there's something special we must do when we interact with spirits. Once you've made the shift, you simply metaphorically lean in and focus intently on the interaction. Trying harder to sense more clearly is counterproductive, because trying causes tension and pulls you out of alpha brain wave state and back to beta.

This doesn't mean there's nothing you can do if you sense no one or drop the link in a connection. You can always re-center yourself with a slow, deep breath, then relax and shift to soul-focus again. Try to trust whatever is happening in the moment.

After you invite a spirit to step into your awareness, consider yourself now in the flow of a natural conversation. Your invitation has initiated this flow, spreading out from your field like ripples on a pond. Those in spirit respond in turn, sending their own ripples of energy-information to merge with yours.

At this point, become like a radar on a boat that continuously scans surrounding waters, sensing every ripple. Passively notice anything you see clairvoyantly, hear clairaudiently, sense clairsentiently, or simply know claircognizantly. Sit calmly and confidently, focusing on your experience, noting every sensation, thought, and feeling.

What stands out?

As you sense anything that is not arising from your own ripples, begin to interact. Switch from passive to active by sending a silent greeting and engage in conversation with whoever has merged with you. Ask questions as appropriate. Flow!

If you are interacting on behalf of someone else, such as a medium does for a client in a private reading, pass along objectively what you are experiencing. In other words, you would report, "I'm sensing, hearing, or seeing this ..." Allow the other person to share your inner experience through your descriptions. This way, even if your subsequent interpretation of what you are experiencing makes no sense to the other person, they might recognize the basic message.

Human beings have a strong tendency to want to be right. This desire can cause you to filter information discerned during a spirit connection. Train yourself to report everything you sense unless it might be hurtful or harmful.

Even if you think you are making something up, by stating all details, you will come to learn through your client's feedback the subtle distinction between your own thoughts and a valid communication. You will also come to trust Spirit and will not miss a gold nugget that would never have come through if you had held back out of fear.

Each interaction, just like every exchange you have with people you know, is unique. Whether in physical form or formless, interactions are dynamic and fluid because all arise from the one shared mind, which is bursting with potential. Expectations and assumptions limit that potential. When you approach mediumship with openness, trust, and a childlike spirit of playfulness, a flow ensues. This can result in outcomes beyond your human imagination.

In the next chapter, I will share with you specific practices you can use to deepen your connection with spirit, which will in turn enhance your ability to receive clear messages for yourself or others.

# PRACTICES TO DEEPEN YOUR SPIRIT CONNECTION

Some people will find that the ability to communicate with the non-physical realms unfolds naturally. But for most, it is a skill that may need to be lovingly coaxed out. Happily, mediumship abilities are innate to all souls and can be developed with commitment and practice.

In the previous section, you learned seven foundational keys to developing mediumship. These keys will help you every time you intend to make a connection with non-physical beings. In this section, you will learn specific practices that will enhance your mediumship journey, no matter your level of ability.

## YOUR VITAL POWER

When we talk about achieving a goal, we often say we have to work at it. What is work? It is the application of force or effort that takes you from one state to another. In mediumship, the work required is to raise your state of consciousness and shift your focus from the human frequency to that of the spirit world.

There are many names for the vital power that flows through your energy field. These include *life force, chi, ki, and prana.* No matter what you call it, this is a very real force. Whether the energy is sluggish or flowing freely and unimpeded will determine how clear your connection is with the higher dimensions.

Life is dynamic—constantly changing—and so is your energy field. Your experiences from moment to moment and the thoughts and feelings that result from these experiences affect the flow of life force energy. This can be a challenge in mediumship if you are not in alignment with your higher self.

The blessing is that with awareness you can tap into your true nature as a beautiful soul. You can instantly take charge of your energy field and upgrade your thoughts and emotions. Each time you do so, you are strengthening your auric field and raising your consciousness.

Each person has a unique energetic signature made up of the vibrations their thoughts and feelings have been radiating throughout their lifetime. I call this your energetic "ringtone." The goal in building your vital power for mediumship is to create and maintain the most harmonious, high-vibration tone possible.

You may be wondering, if there is nothing but life force energy and it already flows through you, then why do you need to build it? Because you are both a soul and human. The activities of daily living in this earthly realm can sap your energy. Interacting with other humans whose energy fields are dissonant to your own can be a drain on your personal vibration. If you do nothing to regularly realign yourself with your power, you might not be maximizing your energetic potential.

Sitting in your vital power, which you will do in this exercise, is akin to a workout for the soul. Just like going to the gym to build your muscles, you can strengthen your aura through repetition—but you can't expect one workout to last a lifetime. If not reinforced through regular exercise, your awareness of and alignment with higher consciousness will dissipate, simply from experiencing life as a human being.

For a medium, it is vitally important to build up a storehouse of this basic energetic fuel. There may be days when you need to make a connection and you aren't feeling particularly strong, emotionally or physically. By regularly building your connection to Spirit with intention, you create a reserve that you can call upon when other resources are running low.

There are any number of ways to raise your vibration, but the most effective will include the following:

- Having clear intention: Each time, as you sit to build your vital power, review why you are doing so. Note your current state of wellbeing and set the intention to balance and increase the flow of any sluggish or stagnant energy.
- Relaxation and silence: Sit quietly and use slow, deep breaths to relax.
- Using visualization to direct the flow of life force energy.

Visualization might be the most important key to strengthening your energy field.

## BUILDING THE POWER

Energy flows in specific patterns throughout your body. A basic exercise to build your vital power will address the vertical flow of yin and yang/feminine and masculine energy through your main energetic axis.

Picture this axis as a shaft or tube of white light that comes down from above you and connects you to the center of the earth, far below your feet.

As you breathe in, visualize yourself pulling in yin—or feminine—energy from below and yang—or masculine energy—from above. Picture these two distinct yet complementary energies coming together at your heart. See if you can sense if one is stronger than the other. Note that imbalances occur frequently, so what you sense might be different each time you do this exercise.

If you become aware of any imbalance, ask for help from the higher realms—from Source, if you will, or the angels—to adjust the flow of yin and yang energy to a state of perfect balance. Notice the difference you feel as you use intention, visualization, and prayer to bring these two main energetic streams into alignment. The results can be instantaneous and stunning.

With the main axis now balanced, move your awareness to the seven energetic centers in the body known as the *chakras*.

It is very helpful to visualize the colors traditionally associated with each chakra as you focus on them sequentially from the base of the spine to the top of your skull:

1st Root Chakra: Red
2nd Sacral Chakra: Orange
3rd Solar Plexus Chakra: Yellow
4th Heart Chakra: Emerald Green
5th Throat Chakra: Pale Blue
6th Third Eye Chakra: Indigo Blue
7th Crown Chakra: Violet

This practice combines focus with clairvoyance, both of which are necessary skills for mediumship. To make this training even more effective, you can go a step beyond visualizing colors and bring clairsentience into the equation. My guides, Sanaya, introduced me to specific qualities of the soul they call The Sacred Seven. These innate characteristics are associated with the chakras as follows:

1st Chakra: Joy
2nd Chakra: Peace

3rd Chakra: Strength

4th Chakra: Courage

5th Chakra: Gratitude

6th Chakra: Humility

7th Chakra: Divine Love

The greater your ability to generate the feeling of these high vibrational qualities as you focus on each chakra, the more you open yourself to your own innate power and sense of wholeness. Pay particular attention to these five chakras which play the most important roles in mediumship:

- The third chakra is the solar plexus and the engine which fuels your connection to the spirit world. It is the seat of your clairsentience— your intuitive sense of knowing and the ability to feel those in spirit. Strength is the quality of the soul associated with this energy center. Your focus on this attribute along with the color yellow as you visualize the solar plexus area will keep you from feeling depleted when working with higher energies.

- The fourth is the heart chakra and the bridge between the physical and non-physical dimensions. While you focus on this chakra, visualize rays of light radiating outward from your heart. These are quite real. As a projection of the one true Light, you are a beacon for the spirit world. When you focus on the heart chakra and the color green as you strengthen your innate courage, you stand out to those in the higher dimensions.

- The fifth is the throat chakra and the seat of your clairaudience. The sixth chakra is the third eye and the seat of your clairvoyance. You will strengthen your ability to both hear and see information from those in spirit as you breathe in the two qualities associated with the 5th and 6th chakras: gratitude and humility. Add in the practice of visualizing the colors associated with each at the same time and you will truly be training your ability to focus while you turn up your innate clairaudience and clairvoyance.

- Strengthening the seventh chakra, the crown allows you to sit in awareness of the self as Divine Love, to breathe in the life force and feel it *as* Love … to come to know yourself as this. Can you imagine how our world would change if everyone did this practice regularly?

After focusing on all seven chakras and visualizing them perfectly balanced, aligned, and pulsating with life force, once again move the power vertically throughout your energy field. Intention and focused thought move consciousness, so it is your thoughts that propel these actual waves of energy. As you become more sensitized to the spirit within, you will physically feel the undulations. You might find yourself rocking gently as the waves flow rhythmically up and down the vertical axis of your etheric body.

If you have never been aware of the movement of energy within you, this physical experience of the power flowing through you can be startling. Always remember that when working with your vital power, you have nothing to fear. This power is the very same light that burned within you long before you took on physical form. Its essence is love, peace, and joy. Surrender to the experience and be transformed as you instinctively remember your true nature.

Keep in mind that each time you sit in your power, the outcome might be different. Do not expect to have earth-shaking, life-changing experiences each time. Opening to the awareness of Spirit is a journey, and your path will unfold perfectly and with Divine timing.

Do these practices to build your power several times a week, as well as any time you are feeling out of balance. The benefits of doing so go far beyond mediumship. Regular strengthening results in less stress, higher physical energy, clearer thoughts, a more focused mind, and a much greater sense of connection with others.

## CREATING A PERSONAL AFFIRMATION

Mediumship is a natural ability, but it may not arise without a little push-back from the many subconscious thoughts that can easily sabotage your best intentions. As you build your trust in the presence and assistance of those in the spirit world, it is helpful to connect with confidence. You can build and strengthen a powerful state of confidence by using affirmations.

It doesn't matter if you fully believe what you are saying when you use positive statements. Your subconscious mind will act on whatever you think and say. Use this fact to your advantage when preparing for spirit communication and consciously create the optimum state in which to work.

Here are affirmations that will serve you well in creating a mediumship mindset:

- I know the spirit world and those in it are real.
- I know that I have the innate ability to connect soul to soul with spirits.
- I am supported by the field created by all the great mediums of the past and present, and I harness this energy now for the best possible connection.
- I trust the intelligence of Source to flow here now and guide this connection, moment by moment.

Can you feel the strength in these words? This higher vibration is what you will radiate as you use similar affirmations with the intention of raising your consciousness. What other words might prove helpful in upgrading your personal belief system?

I recommend that you choose at least three affirmations with which you truly resonate. Write and save them where you can review them as part of your preparations for connecting across the veil. Be sure to feel your affirmations in the heart as you state each one. While rituals are not necessary, the repetition of your personal power phrases has a strengthening effect on the field in which you work each time you practice mediumship.

# JUST ASK

I cannot emphasize strongly enough that you are never alone. Those across the veil want you to know they are here. They are standing by to help you. Too often we forget that we can turn to those in the higher realms to help us. This includes helping you with your mediumship in the following ways.

## ASK FOR EVIDENCE

You have learned in this book how helpful and important evidence is for proving the presence of discarnate souls. The gold nuggets of information you couldn't know can change lives.

If you tell those in spirit the kind of evidence you want them to give you, they will give it to you. I was stunned when my original mentor, Janet Nohavec, shared this in my first class in mediumship. I also found it very comforting. Asking for and receiving specific signs will make spirit communication as reliable and replicable as possible.

If your goal is to do readings for others, I recommend you develop a list of the types of evidence those in spirit might give you when you connect.

Think about the kind of details that would convince a loved one of their presence. The more obvious ones include:

- Male or female
- The age at which they passed
- How they passed
- What type of work they did
- Their name
- Distinct features of their personality
- What they looked like

When I do this practice in a classroom setting, I ask the students to contribute their ideas as we create a reference list together. Even when they think we have thought of every possibility, I always discover additional items that they hadn't thought of, such as:

- Military service
- Pets
- Education level

The purpose of doing this exercise is two-fold. It expands your awareness about the depth of details those in spirit can provide and it opens you to the possibility of receiving these details when you do connect. Of course, the most important things we want to discern from those in spirit are the messages they want to share such as:

- Apologies
- Thank you's
- Things left unsaid
- Expressions of love

A good way to create a truly rich list is to imagine that you are writing the biography of someone who passed. What information would you include about that person to create a full and accurate portrayal of their life?

Put time into developing your list. Make the effort of writing or typing it. When you have what you consider to be as complete a list as possible, sit quietly and read all the items. As you do so, invite angels or your main spirit guide to read along with you. When you get to the bottom, ask that any spirits with whom you communicate from now on will naturally give you as many items on the list as possible, without you having to ask.

Once you put this request out to the spirit world, do your best to not obsess about any item on the list. Review it, as explained above, and then put it away. Your guide and the angels have this! Anticipate with excitement those sacred moments when someone across the veil shares something unexpected and you think, "That's on the list!"

Now that you have asked, trust that just the right evidence will come up when you communicate with those in spirit.

## ASK FOR VALIDATION

Those in spirit know we want to trust that what we are sensing is not our imagination. They understand our doubts that the connection is valid. They want you to know that they are real. To this end, they will do everything in their power to help prove this to you. Therefore, they do not mind when you ask them to validate their presence with evidence and signs.

The first time I connected with my stepdaughter Susan, after years of trying, I heard her words in her own voice. I felt her sweet presence. I had no doubt whatsoever that my efforts had finally paid off. I knew that I would come out of the meditation in which she appeared, and I would tell her father that Susan had visited me. I also knew that my husband would likely placate me with a pat on the shoulder and say, "That's nice, Suzanne."

I wanted Ty to feel the same comfort that I did receiving a visit from our beloved Susan, so I made a special request. I asked her to tell me something about her biological mother that I couldn't possibly know. Susan complied immediately, rattling off three facts that were random and unusual enough that I felt a shiver of excitement.

I knew I would be able to validate this sacred visit with the three details she shared: that her mother's cat was sick, that she had just had an incident with a ladder, and that she currently had Christmas lights inside her house, even though it wasn't Christmas season.

After drying my happy tears, I left my meditation room and shared the big news with Ty. He trusted me and agreed to call his ex-wife. I told her about Susan's visit and asked her to comment on the three items Susan shared in response to my request for validation.

We learned that yes, she had just brought her cat home from the veterinary clinic with medication. Yes, she had been at a wedding the day before and had helped to look for a ladder. And yes, she had white Christmas lights running up the banister of her staircase that she left there year-round.

Way to go, Susan!

An evidential medium always asks for evidence during a reading. Don't hesitate to ask the same of your own loved ones and any higher being who shows up in your meditations. One of the most life-changing experiences occurred for me in meditation one day when I sensed the presence of Jesus. I asked him for validation, and he did something so miraculous that I could no longer deny the deep, spiritual truths that I teach as part of The Awakened Way®.

In addition to asking spirits to validate their visit with evidence, you can also play what I call The Sign Game. Doing so will bring joy and playfulness into your mediumship, not to mention into your daily life.

Anytime you interact with a higher being, if you would like to trust what you discern or you simply want to have fun, ask them, *What sign will you send me as validation that I can trust this?* Remain silent and note the first thing that arises in awareness. It may be a word, a phrase, or an image. Make a mental or written note, and then set it aside. Do not make any special effort to encounter this sign. Trust that what you have perceived will appear within the next few days.

Because those in spirit have a higher perspective, they will project into your mind field something that they can see is coming your way. For example, I recently asked my guides if it was true that there are more angels around us waiting to help than we can imagine. They replied yes. I asked them what sign they would send me to validate their response and I immediately heard the word, *Eureka.*

True validation signs from those across the veil will be unusual but not so rare as to be nearly impossible. In the case of my example, I could not remember the last time I had heard or seen the word *eureka*, but it wasn't outside the realm of possibility. I looked forward with eager anticipation to my eureka moment.

I didn't have to wait long.

The next day, Ty and I received a FedEx shipment with a stone sculpture we had bought on a recent trip. The artist included in the crate a magazine with an article about his work. When I opened the magazine to the page he had marked with one of his brochures, I did a double take and then burst into joyous laughter. The title of the article about the sculptor, written in eye-catching, four-inch-high letters, was *Eureka!*

Can you see that my guides chose something that I was guaranteed to notice? They knew the magazine was already on its way to me.

My guides often have led me to unwittingly stumble upon an anticipated sign. At times, I feel a ramping up of energy as I'm reading a book or magazine that lets me know I will find my sign in the pages ahead. Even though I fully trust our non-physical helpers, these magical moments never fail to leave me gasping with surprise.

I love picturing those in spirit joyously anticipating our delight each time we encounter the signs they have given us. As you make a habit of asking for signs, you, too, will see the web of connections at work. Your joy and feeling of awe when the signs appear will help to maintain the sense of childlike openness that is foundational to connecting with Spirit.

# ENJOYING AHA MOMENTS

Whether you are seeking evidence during a mediumistic encounter or asking for a sign that will appear afterwards, do so from the heart. The more you practice interacting in this way, the more you will come to know how near those in spirit are. You will learn to trust that you are never alone, and you will come to ask for assistance of any kind whenever you need it.

Here is a wonderful practice for helping you to live an awakened, consciously connected, divinely guided life: Pause regularly throughout the day to connect with Spirit. You can do so to receive guidance on the spot, to strengthen your connection with your spirit team, or to simply remind yourself that you are not only human!

I call these brief pauses AHA Moments because AHA is an acronym for the three easy steps involved.

**Align.** Simply take one or more slow, deep breaths to become relaxed and centered. The goal is to achieve a coherent state in body, mind, and spirit. If you don't know what this feels like, simply imagine the opposite of incoherent.

When you note a difference in your state of relaxation and attentiveness, move to the second step: **Harmonize.** Most people can listen to a singer or musical instrument that is out of tune and innately know that it is off key. The same is true when you are out of tune with your true nature as a soul. Harmonizing is as simple as thinking thoughts of love, compassion, gratitude, and any other of the innate qualities of the soul. Don't just think these words—engender the feelings and sensations they represent. In so doing, you will effectively harmonize your energy field.

**Attune.** The second A in AHA is attune. Attune yourself with any higher being who can be of service to you in the moment. You do this by intending to connect with whoever will serve the greatest possible good. Make the vibrational shift beyond your human identity and ask a question for which you don't have an answer. This could be as simple as, "What do I need to know right now?" Then relax and note whatever arises immediately in response to your request. Is it helpful? Give thanks and act on it as appropriate.

The more you pause for AHA Moments, the more you will come to see yourself as an interdependent being who does not have to struggle through life unassisted.

Coming to understand who we really are and how we are never truly disconnected from Spirit provides a solid foundation for developing our own strong communication with higher realms of existence. From that comfortable certainty of knowing, use the tools and practices set forth in this chapter. They will help clarify and enrich this eternal source of guidance, love, and support in our lives.

What a gift!

# FINAL THOUGHTS AND BLESSINGS

*M*ediumship, as a vocation, is one of the healing professions. The potential to alleviate suffering and bring comfort is what makes mediumship sacred work. Whether used for personal or professional purposes, however, the practitioner who strives for constant improvement will reap the rewards of self-healing. This collateral benefit of mediumship arises from the fact that you are regularly working with the higher vibrations of the life force that is Source.

As you work to raise your personal vibration and better merge with the fields of those in spirit, you discover and clear mental, spiritual, and emotional blockages in your own energy field. The insights you gain from the higher realms help you navigate the natural challenges of life with greater peace and balance.

The result is that you find yourself consciously aware of being a soul and living from this elevated perspective far more often than the average human. You integrate this higher state into your day-to-day life and realize that you are divinely guided always, even when your awareness dis-integrates momentarily into "only human" behavior.

The more you allow your true nature to shine through in your human role, the more you fulfill your purpose and experience peace, love, and joy, moment by moment. You come to know that you are already whole and complete at the level of the soul.

If this sounds like a panacea, I assure you it is not. These gifts result from practicing mediumship and coming to know who you truly are. Each encounter you enjoy with those in the non-physical realms increases your awareness that you are *not* only human. You notice the signs and synchronicities that make it clear that you are part of one big web connecting all that is. You come to trust that the force that breathes you is creative, healing, and ever-present.

As you embrace these truths, you navigate the world and its complexities with ease, comfort, and grace. Your mind is open, viewing events from a higher perspective with curiosity and wonder.

Relationships are experienced as an enhancement to your life, regardless of their nature. Your heart is open, seeing yourself and all others from a place of compassion, kindness, and love. You—an eternal soul—are innately magnificent, and you know it. You shine your beautiful light like a beacon into a world that is so greatly in need of hope and encouragement.

The journey of mediumship, like life, is ever onward, ever upward. Because you don't know how wide you can open your personal portal to the higher realms, don't settle for mediocre connections. Those in the spirit world depend on mediums to notice their after death communications and be their voice.

To that end, if you feel a calling in your heart to attune as clearly as possible to spirit, you might want to make this simple checklist part of your spiritual practice:

- Identify any limiting beliefs and replace them with truth.
- Train your mind to be quiet through regular meditative practice.

- Shift your focus often to the higher realms.
- Practice connecting often with spirit beings.
- Ask your guides how you can improve, and then apply what you learn.
- Clear energetic blockages and build the power with regular chakra balancing.
- Read uplifting words daily.
- Be open to all possibilities and play!
- Be the presence of love.

What does this last item have to do with improving mediumship? Everything!

Love is the connective tissue between the physical and non-physical worlds. It is the underlying essence of reality, for in reality, there is only one universe with no separation. This lack of separation is the true definition of love. Mediumship demonstrates that love is what binds us and that true, Divine Love—in its limitless expressions—never dies.

This is what makes mediumship the sacred path that it is: The awareness that love is the force that breathes you and all those with whom you are trying to connect.

It is my desire that you will find in this book and in these practices, the rich blessing of making a solid connection to your loved ones in spirit and your own true essence. In so doing, you can discover healing, freedom, and joy. I offer my blessings and my hope for your success in these efforts.

In the process of making your own clear connection with higher consciousness, remember that you are so very loved, and you are never alone on this journey of life.

# MEET THE SACRED STORYTELLERS

LINDA SERWAY BORDWELL is a retired Speech Language Specialist, educator, writer, and watercolor artist. She is also a wife, a mom, and a grandmother, who is grateful for all the chapters of her well-loved life.

ANNIE BRUNELLI is a student of Suzanne Giesemann, as well as of all things mystical and metaphysical. She is a Spiritual Care volunteer at Celia's House Hospice. Retired in 2019 after many years of living in San Francisco, she is a grateful resident of Ashland, Oregon.

AUDREY BURNS resides in Missouri with her husband, three boys, and eleven pound chihuahua mix. She is a teacher, Reiki Master, retreat leader, and life-long learner.

KELLY BEERS CAPREZ is an evidential medium and psychic. Before fully embracing and developing her spiritual abilities, she was the epitome of the left-brained, logical mind, having worked as an attorney, a biologist, and a local news anchor and reporter. She resides with her husband and three very special children. kellycolettemedium.com.

CELIA CHANTAL, RN is the mother of a beautiful tween, sacred music and sound healer, Hospice RN, and psychic medium living in the Pacific Northwest. She loves uplifting and inspiring fellow creatures to find joy, peace, and healing in this magnificent life. celiachantal.com.

ELIZABETH CLARK is a board certified music therapist who is writing her first book *Healing in the Himalayas* based on her transformative spiritual experience beginning in Nepal.

MARYA CORNELI has had many mystical experiences, messages from the other side, and some spontaneous past life recall. She is learning to trust her intuition. Marya enjoys traveling and has taught English at home and abroad. She is also a Seimei practitioner, a fourth-dimensional healing art from Japan. seimeifoundation.org.

BONNIE EARL dedicated 35 years to the Canadian public education system. After the passing of her husband and dad, she felt compelled to share life lessons and prove communication across the veil exists. Her passion is to be part of a global consciousness-expanding community bringing messages of hope to those struggling. bonnie-earl.com.

MELINDA ESPARZA lives and paints in the desert Southwest. She seeks to learn more about Spirit and more about the Source of all that is. She is the stepdaughter of James Todd.

CHENÉE FOURNIER is an evidential medium and energy healer who is honored to provide evidence that life continues beyond our physical existence.

**SAUNDRA GATTIE** is a loving mother with two children, one in spirit. She is on a never-ending healing journey while trying to spread the word of the afterlife and our eternal love.

**ROXANNE HUPP** is a chemical engineer turned leader who coaches others to see their full potential. She has a strong passion for learning with a compassionate emphasis on mentoring.

**CELESTE HUTTES** is a freelance writer who lives in Central Illinois with her fur babies, Bindi and Emerson. She enjoys exploring alternative healing methods and life's big questions.

**AMBER KASIC** is an evidential medium and teacher in the field of education. She writes and speaks about her shared death experience with her father and its journey of healing, forgiveness, and personal transformation. She inspires others to explore just what is possible in our lives, as love is limitless. natureswayopen.com.

**MARY JANE KLOCKE** is a native of Iowa. She has spent her adult life working for a corporation in various cities. For the past 16 years she has been happily married and happily retired in Florida. She enjoys gardening, golfing, and growing spiritually.

**MELISSA KNUTSON** is the proud mother of two beautiful souls, Cale and Hannah. View the Goosebump Moments video *Hug from Heaven*, to see the hug from her story.

**BARBARA STRAUS LODGE** is an essayist whose writings have appeared in The Los Angeles Times, Huffington Post, The Rumpus Voices of Addiction, Chicken Soup for the Soul, Parabola Magazine, New York Times,

Motherlode, and a variety of anthologies. She is the author of *A Call for Kindness, Connection, and Science* published in the Journal of Substance Abuse Treatment. barbarastrauslodge.com.

SUSAN LYNCH is the mother of two adult sons in spirit and the author of her award-winning memoir, *Life After Kevin*. Susan spreads hope by writing and speaking about healing after loss due to an overdose or suicide. susan-lynch. com.

IRINA MELNIK, MD is a non-surgical orthopedics specialist from Stanford, specializing in regenerative and spinal injections procedures. Beyond her medical expertise, she's a spiritual seeker, author, inventor, and world explorer alongside her beloved husband, Dan. Her podcast is *Cures Remedies and Beyond*. comprehensivespineandsports.com.

ANN MICHELE has been a fitness trainer for much of her life. Now 65, she is disabled following a surgical mishap and lives quietly with her partner John. Her main joy is connecting with her two sons in spirit.

PAMELA NANCE, MA, has researched the survival of consciousness after death, is certified in healing touch, past life regression, hypnotherapy, shamanism, spiritual dowsing and has a graduate degree in anthropology.

MARY NARAYA is a spiritual seeker and student who loves nature and exploring the mysteries. She has been a Reiki practitioner and teacher for thirteen years.

LEAH POLASCHEK is a single mom, children's book author, animal lover, and tarot enthusiast who drives a minivan and can't stay up past 10:30 at night.

**SUSAN FERLING POOLE'S** life completely changed when she quit drinking and returned to her roots of intuition and knowing that there is more to life than we are led to believe. Susan feels every day is a blessing and an adventure.

**MARIA DOUGLAS ROSSO'S** life has been filled with no other explanation events. This is a favorite one involving her dad.

**DR. SHARON SASS** is a writer, painter, and psychologist. After her first spiritual experience in her teens, she has studied and been enamored with all things spiritual.

**MARIE SCIVETTI** is a mystic and an aspiring author. Cancer taught her that even in life's darkest, most challenging moments we can rise like the phoenix on wings of grace. Marie hopes to inspire others to embrace these transformational moments and the gifts they bestow.

**SHANNON SHADE** is a registered clinical hypnotherapist based in Calgary, Alberta, Canada. She specializes in evidence-based and trauma-informed hypnotherapy, empowering individuals to enhance their overall well-being.

**JIM SPRUELL** is a musician, artist, writer, and video director. He and his wife lost their beloved son Dakota in 2021.

**WENDY WILLOW** is an intuitive palm reader, numerologist, speaker, and published writer, who has given readings at various psychic and alternate health fairs across Canada and the United States.

# MEET THE AUTHOR

Suzanne Giesemann is a metaphysical teacher, author, and Messenger of Hope, recognized on the Watkins' list of the 100 Most Spiritually Influential Living People. She is a former U.S. Navy Commander who served as a commanding officer and as aide to the Chairman of the Joint Chiefs of Staff. Today, she guides people to the awareness of a greater reality.

Suzanne is a bestselling author of 15 books, 6 Hemi-Sync recordings, and YouTube videos with over ten million views. She produces the Awakened Way app and hosts the popular Messages of Hope podcast. Her gift of multidimensional communication has been verified by noted afterlife researchers, and her messages bring not only hope, but healing and love that go straight to the heart.

Learn more at suzannegiesemann.com.

Printed in the USA
CPSIA information can be obtained
at www.ICGtesting.com
LVHW052029011024
792660LV00001B/1